ESKRIMA

Filipino Martial Art

ESKRIMA
Filipino Martial Art

Krishna Godhania

THE CROWOOD PRESS

First published in 2010 by
The Crowood Press Ltd
Ramsbury, Marlborough
Wiltshire SN8 2HR

www.crowood.com

This impression 2014

British Library Cataloguing-in-Publication Data
A catalogue record for this book is available from the British Library.

ISBN 978 1 84797 152 4

Photographic Acknowledgements:
The instructional photographs were taken by Scott Benzie, the cover
photographs were taken by Juan Antonio Tabernero (aka Kometa), and
the photographs taken in the Philippines were supplied by Noel Perkins.

Disclaimer
Please note that the author and the publisher of this book are not
responsible in any manner whatsoever for any loss, damage, injury or
adverse outcome of any kind that may result from practising, or
applying, the principles, ideas, techniques and/or following the
instructions/information described in this publication. Since the physical
activities described in this book may be too strenuous in nature for some
readers to engage in safely, it is essential that a doctor be consulted
before undertaking training.

Typeset by Jean Cussons Typesetting, Diss, Norfolk

Printed and bound in India by Replika Press Pvt. Ltd.

Contents

Dedication

To my parents, Keshav and Liri Godhania, for encouraging me to study the martial arts and for the sacrifices they made to give me a good life.

To my Eskrima teacher, Grandmaster Abner Pasa, for sharing his personal art, and for the countless hours of happiness, joy and laughter gained from 'playing' Eskrima.

To my wife Deepa, without whose encouragement and support this book would never have seen completion.

To my students: the future of the art – your support continues to help keep it alive.

Acknowledgements

First of all, I would like to thank Sifu Shaun Rawcliffe (Wing Chun Kung Fu) for originally recommending me to Crowood.

Sincere appreciation to my long-time training partner Graham Lawrence, for his invaluable suggestions regarding content, and for editing the manuscript into a more reader-friendly form.

Many thanks to my Eskrima teacher Abner Pasa, for contributing the superb chapter on Eskrima philosophy.

Respect to my students, Darren Moore, Dion Trigg and Michelle Trigg for their technical expertise and assistance with the photographic sequences.

Salutations to Scott Benzie for the excellent instructional photographs that form the bulk of this book, and salutations to Juan Antonio Tabernero (aka Kometa) for the superb cover shots.

Thank you to my student Noel Perkins for supplying copies of photographs taken in the Philippines.

I also have to thank Eskrimador and hugely talented artist Orville Visitacion for the superb life-like illustrations in Chapter 12.

And to Rafael Kayanan for the wonderful body outlines used to construct the template diagrams.

Finally, sincere appreciation for the excellent template diagrams that were constructed by student and friend Francisco 'Paco' Gomez.

Preface

The purpose of this book is to give readers a detailed insight into the Filipino martial art of Eskrima: I hope it inspires them to contact a qualified instructor (guro); and for those already actively involved in the practice of the art, I hope it will inspire them to look in more detail at the system they use, and to further research it. The training methodology, principles and concepts are predominantly from the 'Warriors Eskrima System', founded by Grandmaster Abner Pasa.

As the lineage holder of this system, I have continued to evolve it by introducing new training methods, and by organizing the original techniques and training drills into a progressive and structured curriculum.

The Filipino martial arts are highly evolved and massive in scope, and to go into detail in each area of Eskrima is beyond the scope of this book. However, this is by far the most complete and detailed work on the subject that has been published to date in the UK.

The bulk of the book goes into detail concerning the techniques, drills, training principles and concepts in the following areas: single stick, knife defence, empty hands, double stick, stick and dagger, and staff, with supplementary chapters on flexible weapons, projectiles and training with equipment.

The history chapter contains extremely rare and previously unpublished photos of Eskrima Masters and Grandmasters; and the chapter on philosophy sheds light on a relatively unknown aspect of Eskrima.

Finally, the chapter on self-defence and the law discusses important considerations for the martial artist with regard to the use of 'reasonable force'. Unfortunately, battles don't always end on the street, and often continue into the courtroom, therefore knowledge of the law must be a part of a martial artist's education.

Krishna Godhania
May 2009
Warwick, England.

LEFT: Map of the
Philippines.

BELOW: The Battle of
Mactan (1521).

1 Eskrima – History and Evolution

What is the early history of Eskrima? The answer is that nobody knows for sure. Unfortunately, there are no written treatises on Eskrima before the later part of the twentieth century, and subsequently the history has largely been handed down through oral tradition.

The region known as Visayas (Central Philippines), and in particular Cebu, is widely regarded as the cradle of Eskrima. It was in nearby Mactan Island that the local chieftain Lapu Lapu and his men repelled the Spanish conquistadors in 1521. Ferdinand Magellan, the Portuguese navigator who led the expedition on behalf of the King of Spain, paid with his life at the battle of Mactan. It is believed that Lapu Lapu's men fought with spears, swords and sharpened sticks, and this is the first reference to the existence of the ancient art of Eskrima. The painting (*see* p. 8) shows Lapu Lapu about to apply the 'finishing stroke' to Magellan.

Before the coming of the Spaniards, Eskrima was most likely an art of war taught to warriors to use in the constant tribal wars of that period. Being an art of war, each tribe would evolve its own distinctive techniques based on the type of weapon it preferred, and the environment it lived in. Understandably, each tribe would jealously guard its techniques, strategies and tactics. During this period Eskrima could be classified as a tribal fighting art.

Eventually the Spanish conquered the Philippines, largely through the church, and this Spanish colonization radically changed the practice of Eskrima. To minimize future revolts the warrior class was outlawed, as was the carrying of bladed weapons. The Eskrima *Maestros* (Masters) were forced to take their styles underground, and this involved training with rattan sticks instead of swords, and teaching private pupils who were either members of their own families, or select students who had specifically sought out the Masters.

The techniques of the various styles and systems prevalent during the 1600–1800s would have continued to be closely guarded, as these were centuries of personal duels. Also, *Maestros* would have had to have kept a low profile to avoid attracting the attention of the Spanish authorities.

It is believed that Jose Rizal, Antonio Luna, Juan Luna, Marcelo H. del Pilar and other Filipino exiles working in Spain in the late 1880s for Philippine independence studied fencing. Fencing was often a term used to refer to Eskrima – in fact the French word for fencing is *escrimé*, and the Spanish equivalant is *esgrima*.

However, revolts spreading the gospel of freedom continued to occur over subsequent centuries. The most significant of these was the formation of the secret society for Filipino Independence known as the *Katipunan* (the Brotherhood) in 1896; leading figures in this organization such as Andreas Bonifacio were reputedly Eskrimadors.

After gaining independence from the Spanish in the late 1890s, the Masters slowly started to go public with their styles, with an emphasis on individual 'self defence'.

Eskrima in Cebu

The earliest records of a martial arts association are from 14 August 1920, the year in which the Labangon Fencing Association was organized. The association was formed by a group of *eskrimadors* (practitioners) who practised different styles of Eskrima, but recognized that they could benefit by sharing their knowledge. The Masters of that club all resided in Labangon, a district of Cebu City, hence the name Labangon Fencing Association.

The style of Eskrima most commonly used at that time was still the long blade- (sword-) orientated style. The famous families of eskrimadors in Cebu at that time were the Saavedra (Labangon), Romo (Pasil) and Ilustrisimo (Daan Bantayan). Other lesser known fighters such as Pablo Alicante, who resided in Toledo, were also regarded as being amongst the best.

The Labangon Fencing Club had been formed with the aim of unifying eskrimadors into one group, but this proved to be difficult. The problem of personalities, and whose personal style was the best, soon forced the club into constant conflict. The club was sometimes referred to as the 'club

Eskrima legend Venancio 'Ansiong' Bacon.

Balintawak self-defence club (1952).

of cats and dogs' ('*iro ug iring*'), because as one practitioner was exhibiting his style, the others would be criticizing him. When he finished, someone else would begin to suffer the same treatment.

The club was officially closed due to financial discrepancies by a vote in a board meeting, according to the late Grandmaster Eulogio Canete who was the secretary of the club at that time. The association officially ended on 14 August 1930 – it had survived for exactly a decade.

Two years later, the Doce Pares (Twelve Pairs) club was formed. The name of the club was chosen from a group of fighting men in France who were all expert swordsmen, during the reign of Charlemagne. The club was to have begun in December 1931, but it lacked the desired number of people (twenty-four) to start, and subsequently began on 11 January 1932. Many of the eskrimadors who had been in the Labangon Fencing Association continued their training by joining the new club.

The first Grandmaster of the club was Lorenzo Saavedra, while the top fighter of the club was his nephew, Teodoro 'Doring' Saavedra. Another notable who was involved with the club was the knife specialist Jesus Cui. The Saavedras taught and influenced future greats such as Venancio 'Ansiong' Bacon, Filemon 'Momoy' Canete and Eulogio 'Yoling' Canete.

Other teachers of the Canetes were their father Gregorio and Uncle Pedro. Eulogio also studied with Lieutenant Tinyente Piano Aranas – one of the best and most feared eskrimadors in San Fernando, Cebu. The other top fighters in the San Fernando area were Juanso Tekya, Andres Suarez, Tito de Gama and Cesario Aliason.

It is not clear whether the Doce Pares club was also known as the 'Cebu School of Self Defense', or if this school was an offshoot of Doce Pares. The school taught fencing, jiu-jitsu, wrestling and physical culture.

It is interesting to note that Filipinos were cross-training in Japanese martial arts (jiu jitsu) as early as the 1930s, and this was to continue further after World War II, when

Filipinos trained in such arts as judo and karate.

When the Japanese invaded the Philippines, many Eskrima Masters enlisted into the army and were part of the Bolo Battalion. Bolo is the common term used in the Philippines to refer to a short sword, similar in size to a machete; this was the primary weapon of this battalion, and hence the name. The Filipinos would engage the Japanese in the Philippine jungles, where they were able to use the bolo to great effect. Some soldiers would engage the Japanese in a 'triangle' formation, with the best fighter at the 'point' of the triangle; it was his job to first engage the enemy, whilst the other two would watch his back, and were responsible for 'finishing off' the enemy. A lot of the 'point men' were Eskrima Masters.

Others fought as guerilla fighters, utilizing their combat skills in close quarter skirmishes with the Japanese. But with war comes casualties on both sides, and a number of Eskrima Masters lost their lives, amongst them the legendary Doring Saavedra (who was captured and killed by the Japanese kempe-tai); this left a void in the Doce Pares, although it regrouped with Ansiong Bacon as its top fighter. Unfortunately, personalities and politics soon divided the club. As a result, Ansiong Bacon left and founded the Balintawak Self Defense Club (*see* p. 11). He later went on to train such notables as Delfin Lopez, Teofilo Velez, and Jose Villasin.

Seated on the first row, second from the left is Delfin Lopez, third from the left is Venancio Bacon, and seated third from the right is Jesus Cui.

Meanwhile, the Doce Pares Club was kept alive by the Canete family, with Eulogio and Momoy Canete as the chief instructors, and Ciriaco 'Cacoy' Canete and Vicente 'Inting' Carin as its top fighters. Challenges were common, and a strong rivalry ensued between these clubs for some years. In mid-August 1952 these two fighters organized a self-defence club known as the San Nicolas Mutual Security Association (SANIMUSA) – the name was later changed to CEMUSA.

In 1959, Gerardo 'Larry' Alcuizar (a student of Fernando Candawan, who in turn was a student of Momoy Canete) founded the Durex (Excalibur) Self Defense Club at the Cebu Institute of Technology, where in addition to Eskrima he offered instruction in Combat Judo and Tang Soo Do.

During the 1960s, interest in the Filipino arts increased substantially as more schools and styles opened up to the public. In 1966, Florencio Roque founded the Tornado Garote Self Defense Club to promote the Bahad or Juego Todo (no holds barred) style, made popular by Doring Saavedra.

The 1970s proved yet another important decade in the growth and spread of martial arts in the Philippines. In 1972, Felimon Caburnay, a former sparring partner of Momoy Canete, founded the Lapunti Self Defense Club, 'Lapunti' being an acronym of three barrios in Cebu – Labangon, Punta and Tisa. This style is known for its rapid Abaniko (fanning) strikes, and was later known as Lapunti Arnis de Abaniko.

Later in the same year, Napolean Fernandez founded the art of Yaw Yan, a Filipino kicking style similar to Thailand's Muay Thai. In 1973, Magdeleno Nolasco founded the Black Cat Self Defense Club, where he taught judo and Eskrido – the personal style of Cacoy Canete.

In 1975, Crispulo 'Ising' Atillo formed the Philippine Arnis Confederation. Atillo, who learnt the art from his father, and Venancio Bacon later participated in the infamous duel with Ciriaco Canete in 1983. Also in 1975, Artemio Paez, Felipe Atillo and Carlos Navarro founded the Punta Princesa Eskrima Club. Paez and Navarro would later go on to form the Black Eagle Eskrima Club. In 1977, Florencio Lasola founded the Oolibama Arnis Club in the Talisay area of Cebu.

Those Filipinos who cross-trained in the Japanese or Korean arts quickly learned that

Grandmasters gathering (1987). *LEFT TO RIGHT:* Abner Pasa, Eulogio Canete, Ciriaco Canete, Arnulfo Mongcal, Teofilo Velez, Prudencio Caburnay, Vicente Carin, Jose Mena, Antonio Ilustrisimo, Dionisio Canete.

it takes organization and continuous publicity to popularize a martial art. Some styles started to adopt uniforms, a belt ranking structure, and structured curriculums. At some time in the late 1970s the term 'Grandmaster' was adopted to represent the head of a particular system.

From the mid-1970s onwards the tournament, or 'Sport Arnis', grew in popularity, and organizations such as Naraphil and Arnis Philippines were formed.

So as to keep some of the older traditional styles alive, Abner Pasa formed the Institute of Filipino Martial Arts in the late 1980s, the aim being to expose interested practitioners to teachers of the lesser known traditional and classical styles of Eskrima.

Although Cebu is known as the 'cradle of Eskrima' in the Philippines, there are some similarities and connections with Eskrima on the other Visayan islands, particularly the island of Negros, located to the north-west of Cebu.

Arnis in Negros

Oral tradition tells us that when the Sri Visayans came to the central Visayan islands, some other Datus (chiefs) went to the island of Panay, where they taught and popularized the art. One famous eskrimador, 'Tatay' Isko, who was a member of the Pulahan Rebellion against the Spanish at the end of the last century, moved from Panay to Negros and is believed to have taught some of the better known Negros fighters. Iloilo City (Negros Oriental) at one point in time was a melting pot of Filipino teachers; many of these later relocated to either Bacolod City or Manila.

Bacolod City (Negros Occidental) also has a rich history of Arnis. In 1932, Jose Vinas founded the Lapu Lapu Arnis Aficionados; this made his club, along with Doce Pares, amongs the oldest in the Philippines.

Sisoy Gyabros formed the Bacolod Arnis Club in 1956; Sisoy along with Mang Karpo was regarded as the top fighter of his time amongst the Negros Arnis community. This club only remained active for two years, but produced such notables as Juan Lawan, Frederico Serfino Snr and Amador Chavez. Chavez later went on to establish his own group in 1959.

In 1960, Romeo Mamar founded the art of Tapado. This art utilizes a short staff and is renowned for its power. The art in a basic sense uses only two movements; these are quite often simultaneous blocks and strikes. Mamar developed this style after an extensive study of other long-stick styles such as Lagas, Uhido, Layaw and Sinamak.

Eskrima Outside the Philippines

Many of the Eskrima Masters worked as sailors, or cooks on ships that travelled to various ports around the world. In search of adventure and better economic prospects, many of them 'jumped ship' and resided in Hawaii or Southern California. Floro Villabrille became a legendary figure in the Hawaii Eskrima community, and Eskrima Grandmasters such as Juanito 'John' Lacoste, Leo Giron and Angel Cabales were largely responsible for propagating Eskrima in Stockton, California.

Eskrima came to the UK in 1975, when Rene Latosa, an eskrimador from Stockton, California, first introduced the art to the public. Later, in 1979, Dan Inosanto introduced his Filipino Kali blend, which soon gained a prominent following. However, it was not until 1990 that the Masters who resided in the Philippines started to visit the UK to share their approach to the arts.

The 1990s saw the introduction of stick-fighting tournaments, known as Sport Arnis, and wider publicity of the Filipino martial arts in martial arts magazines and the media.

Nowadays, the Filipino martial arts are practised throughout the world. Modern technology such as the internet has certainly made the world a smaller place, and it is now easier to locate teachers around the globe than ever it has been in the past.

History and Development of Sport Arnis

The popular styles of Eskrima/Arnis that are currently taught and practised today can be classified into traditional (combative) and competitive (sport). Traditional Eskrima places emphasis on classical teaching methodology. This involves learning the *Abecedario*, *amara*, *numerada*, disarming and so on, eventually progressing to two-person flow drills, and finally freestyle sparring. Emphasis is placed on developing a sound defence in addition to effective striking capabilities. In the golden era of Eskrima, when challenge matches were fought without the use of armour, the yardstick by which an eskrimador's level of skill was judged was through his ability to avoid being hit.

It was a common sight in the Philippines to see a proven eskrimador demonstrating his level of proficiency at fiestas. He would place three coconut halves on the floor, balance himself on them, and invite bystanders to attack him. The objective was to defend himself without once losing his balance – and he rarely lost.

Sport Arnis may look like combative Eskrima to the uninitiated, but it is an entirely different thing. The emphasis has shifted largely from defensive to offensive. In fact, it is common to see people who have barely practised the art, but are physically very fit, join tournaments and become 'overnight' champions.

In 1975, an organization named Naraphil (National Arnis Association of the Philippines) was formed under the leadership of General Fabian Ver, then the chief of state of the armed forces of the Philippines. Its objective was to unite the various clubs and eskrimadors throughout the Philippines.

Towards this end a decree was issued by the then president, Ferdinand Marcos, to include the teaching of Arnis in the educational system.

On 24 March 1979, the first open Arnis tournament was sponsored and held by Naraphil in Cebu City; it was well attended, and the Masters' division was dominated by top eskrimador Ciriaco 'Cacoy' Canete. Later, in August of the same year, Naraphil sponsored the first national invitational Arnis tournament in Manila. Once again a Masters' division was held; among those who fought were Cacoy Canete (Doce Pares), Timoteo Maranga (Balintawak), Jose Mena (Doblete Rapillon), Benjamin Lema (Lightning Scientific Arnis) and Florencio Pecate (Pecate Arnis). Cacoy Canete went on to win this division, too.

However, various other Masters who were invited did not fight; among these was the famous Antonio Ilustrisimo. They refused to compete under the tournament's rules, feeling that the restrictions imposed for safety purposes made the whole thing unrealistic. In fact Illustrisimo once said, 'If anyone wants to take my reputation, they will have to fight me with a sword': unsurprisingly there were no challengers.

In the 1980s, the sponsoring of tournaments gained momentum, with the aim of further establishing Arnis as a sport. To this effect, on 16 March 1985, the third national Arnis tournament was held in Cebu City, and the fourth national Arnis was held in Bacolod City on 26 July 1986.

In 1987, after the first international instructor's camp in Cebu city, the World Eskrima-Kali-Arnis Federation (WEKAF) was founded; Dionisio 'Diony' Canete became its first president. It was hoped that with the influence of Western memberships world championships could be held. This materialized on 11–13 August 1989, when WEKAF sponsored the first World Championships in Cebu City. It continues to hold world championships every two years.

In 1991, Arnis Philippines became the 'official' organization (in that it had the backing of the government) to promote and popularize the art of Arnis. Later it went on to become the thirty-third member of the Philippine Olympic Committee. Through this organization's efforts Arnis was featured as a demonstration sport in the 1991 South-East Asian Games (SEA Games). Arnis Philippines then formed the International Arnis Federation, which brought thirty countries together to work towards the acceptance of Arnis as a demonstration sport in the Olympic Games. With Arnis now the national sport of the Philippines, the Senate Committee on Youth and Sports Development, the Philippine Sports Commission and the Philippine Olympic Committee jointly sponsored and endorsed the Grand Exhibition of Martial Arts in Manila.

Types of Sport Arnis

The introduction of rules, which are necessary to limit injury and to increase spectator interest, has made Sport Arnis a game, and like any other game, its operation is greatly influenced by the rules. There are several types of tournament today, one using padded sticks while the competitors fight with minimal protective gear, and the other whereby rattan sticks are used with the use of full body armour. One format recognizes the first hit as the means of determining points, while another awards the decision to the player who delivers the highest number of strikes for the duration of the bout.

Both formats have their advantages and disadvantages. In the first format, padded sticks are used to resemble a blade or a very heavy stick – weapons that could very well finish a fight with a well placed powerful blow. Subsequently, points are awarded to the first strike that scores. This format can be boring from a spectator's point of view, because the referee will quite often stop the fight and restart it; thus, one will rarely see a spectacular exchange of blows – 'toe to toe' in this format. Because it has minimal spectator interest, this format is less popular. However, if conducted properly it has an advantage in that the minimal protective gear worn – usually headgear and gloves – obliges the player to develop good defensive skills. If he does not, he will feel a well placed strike.

The second method involves wearing a body protector in addition to the headgear and hand protection, and is the most popular today. It is a good method to introduce a student to full contact sparring, as the safety gear helps remove inhibitions and encourages the student to be aggressive when fighting. Since this format scores on the highest number of hits, the style of play is attacking by comparison. This format can look spectacular and is, therefore, more popular with spectators; as a result it is the preferred format for most tournaments.

However, there are some disadvantages with this approach. First, the padding can encourage the player to become complacent and neglect his defence, and in the process absorb blows that could render him unconscious in a real fight. Furthermore, many techniques are banned in the interest of safety; these include thrusts, *punyo* strikes, and punching with the live hand and leg sweeps, and the exclusion of these techniques can make the player vulnerable to such manoeuvres if he is not familiar with them.

Currently the various organizations are still fine-tuning a scoring format, and the referee has two concerns: to judge the technical expertise of the players while maintaining spectator interest. This involves striking a balance between good defensive capabilities and non-stop striking and showmanship. Perhaps a system of awarding greater points to strikes delivered to vital points should be considered; doing so would force the player to exhibit accuracy and skill in the delivery of their strikes, as opposed to hitting anywhere. Considering these options will mean that the days of a champion who is merely superior in fitness but not in skill will be eradicated, in turn bringing together the skills of the traditional art with a transfer of skill to the sporting arena.

Conclusion

Since the late 1980s there has been a steady increase in the number of foreigners travelling to study Eskrima or Arnis in the Philippines. The stick-fighting tournaments have been a big draw, but the increase in publicity from television, and also Hollywood, have helped stimulate greater interest in the Filipino arts.

The first television programme to seriously showcase Eskrima in the Philippines was the BBC's *Way of the Warrior* (1982), and in more recent years there was the BBC's *Mind, Body and Kick Ass Moves*.

Regarding movies, following the Bruce Lee boom in the 1970s, a film was made in Cebu called *Enter the Garote*, translated as *Enter the Stick*; it featured many of the Filipino Masters mentioned in this chapter. In the United States, Dan Inosanto appeared in numerous films throughout the 1980s exhibiting aspects of the Filipino martial arts.

In more recent years, films such as *The Hunted* and the *Jason Bourne Trilogy* had fight scenes based on techniques and movements from the Filipino Martial Arts.

2 Principles and Concepts

Introduction

Martial arts are always structured around certain principles and concepts, and some instructors may sometimes talk about these without necessarily explaining to the student exactly what is meant.

A **principle** may refer to a rule of personal conduct – for example, you never start a fight – or to a fundamental law or basic truth, or assumed truth, which may be a guide to action. If you push someone, they are naturally inclined to push back rather than to give way. This is an observed principle, which you may be able to take advantage of.

A **concept** is the expression of an idea, in the sense of a generalized or abstract idea. It may be inferred or derived from specific observations, but the concept itself is on a higher level than having only one application or relating to only one observation. If you are aware of using a distraction to create an opening (to create a possible target for a strike), that is a concept, because it is a general idea. If you use distraction 1 to create opening 1, and distraction 2 to create opening 2, then you are using the concept, but within two different specific techniques. Neither of the techniques is the concept: the concept underlies both of those techniques, and many others.

If you unbalance someone, the focus of their attention will immediately be on recovering their balance before they can think about hitting you. That is a principle, a fundamental observed truth as a guide to action. For the martial artist, it is the act of unbalancing an opponent, which then becomes a useful concept, and that can be achieved through a number of different methods such as pulling, pushing, tripping, kicking, head manipulations – all different methods of employing the *concept* of unbalancing, to make use of the *principle* of the fact that while he is unbalanced, you are in control of your next action, but he is not: whether trained or not, his subconscious mind and his body's own receptive sense will be absorbed with recovering control of balance, because of the basic danger presented to the organism by the act of falling.

The concepts of a martial art are therefore more important than the specific techniques, because they can be applied in different and creative ways to achieve the same desired ends. It is therefore more important to understand what you are trying to achieve and why, rather than *how* to do one or more specific techniques – although the 'how' is still the necessary first step, as this introduces the student to practical means of applying important concepts before they can acquire a higher level of understanding, giving them flexibility and adaptability rather than 'more techniques'.

Eight Fundamental Principles

After decades of study and reflection, my Eskrima teacher, Grandmaster Abner Pasa, developed the following eight fundamental principles (in alphabetical order):

1. Appropriateness.
2. Awareness.
3. Balance.
4. Characteristic of Tool.
5. Nature of the Environment.
6. Objectiveness.
7. Skilfulness.
8. Universality.

I am going to look at three of these principles in this chapter, but please refer to Chapter 12 (written by Abner Pasa) for a more detailed explanation of all eight principles.

Awareness
The first principle of self-defence is nothing to do with physical fighting skills at all, but is awareness. You should generally be alert to your surroundings, rather than going around in a distracted frame of mind, with your attention focused internally instead of on your environment.

This does not require you to develop a paranoid sense of immediate and ever-present danger. It simply means being aware that dangerous situations are possible, and that they are often (though not always) indicated – for instance, there is an argument going on, or someone is becoming increasingly angry. It might be time to calm down or say something different, or to distract someone. It might look like time for you to cross the street and walk in the other direction, rather than heading towards that group of people up ahead.

It might mean cultivating the habit of not walking next to walls where there are dark alleyways, and not walking around looking at the ground. If you perhaps look like a depressed victim, oblivious to danger, you can be a magnet to a potential mugger. If you have a confident and determined stride, and simply look as if you know where you are going and what is happening around you, the mugger is likely to look for a victim elsewhere.

It might mean making extremely basic decisions, such as not getting into an unmarked taxi outside the pub at 1 o'clock in the morning; or perhaps making sure that you are never outside a pub or nightclub in the early hours of the morning anyway, as this is a frequent time and place for drunken brawls and thieves and other dangerous situations.

All of that is about sensible awareness, and will keep you out of a lot more trouble than learning some self-defence techniques.

When faced by a threat, are you aware of possible escape routes? If you are being threatened by someone, have you seen a weapon? If you have not, are you aware of where he might draw one from? The best strategy for increasing the statistical likelihood of your success, escape and survival is to assume that if you haven't seen a weapon, he has one; that if you *have* seen a weapon, he has *another* one; and that if you have seen only one attacker, there is *somebody* else about to turn up to help him.

If there is already more than one attacker, is it possible to position yourself so that they get in each other's way, so that you can use one of them as a shield between you and the others? When fear increases your adrenalin flow, regard it as your friend: use it to increase your strength and speed, not to reduce your awareness and give you 'tunnel vision' so that one person distracts you while another one hits you from the side.

There are times when, no matter how sensible and aware you have been, you are unlucky enough to be in a situation where someone wants to hurt you. When you have no choice, your martial arts training takes over. Before that, however, there are many times when you *would* have had a choice, perhaps between injury and escape, if only you had been sufficiently aware.

The Nature of the Environment

In order to understand the development of a fighting art, one needs to analyse the environment in which it evolved. The environment in the Philippine Islands differs greatly, depending on where you are. For example, while travelling in northern Luzon, an area where rice fields dominate the landscape, I noticed that a linear type of system was more prevalent in this region. According to Abner Pasa:

> The rice field is characterized by narrow and slippery pathways. The layout of those pathways is linear, and at points where one

pathway crosses another it is angular. As a result, the styles in this type of environment are characterized by low, stable stances. Reinforced blocking is predominant, and evading blows is usually done with body angling, such as slipping, ducking or swaying. Footwork is minimal, for fear of losing one's balance on the slippery terrain.

In the Western Visayas, such as Negros Occidental, the landscape is flatter and wider open. As a result the staff (long stick) is a popular weapon in this region, whereas in heavily wooded areas the short stick is more popular.

Environmental training – rice fields. Grandmaster Pacifico 'Pacs' Taneo.

Environmental training – sugar-cane fields.

In some parts of Mindanao the terrain is characterized by narrow paths with heavy underbrush growth on the sides; and the means of travelling is through narrow bamboo footbridges. In this type of environment, the styles tend to rely heavily on thrusts, known as '*tutsada*', as opposed to slashing. The reason for this is, if you miss with a slash, your weapon may get trapped in the underbrush growth, while thrusting would minimize this risk.

Other traditional methods of environmental training in the Filipino martial arts are:

• training on sand;
• training in low light;
• training on the stairs;
• training in a doorway.

I feel it is very important to practise your art in different environmental conditions, as this will force you to *adapt* your style to any environment.

The practice of techniques in one training environment is insufficient to instil a well rounded ability to respond in different circumstances. The normal training environment is usually clear, well roofed and well lit. The repetition of technique in the usual gym or *dojo* will indeed lead to the acquisition of appropriate body mechanics, timing, coordination, footwork, sensitivity and reactions.

However, what will be the circumstances in which you are called upon to use your skills for self-defence? You could be on a strange street, tired and suffering from a virus, and suddenly under the influence of the fear of a threat. You may be alone, with a friend, or with a crowd, or with a child or an attractive member of the opposite sex who is perceived as a desirable target by one or more attackers. Can you use your skills while dealing with the distractions of having to avoid or protect other untrained individuals?

Do you always train techniques for one-on-one attacks? What happens when you have to try and deal with two or more attackers? This is extremely difficult, and training must occasionally include 'zoning' footwork and 'shielding' strategy for such situations. It can also be a good idea to place physical obstacles around the training area, in case you are in a position where you need to manoeuvre around objects (or use them for protection, or as self-defence tools or distractions).

What if it is raining, or muddy? What happens to your strategies and footwork, and balance and kicking skills? What if it is dark or you are injured? Do you deliberately explore the use of some of your training drills or techniques with an 'artificial' inhibition, such as only being able to use either your right or your left hand instead of both, or practising drills in low light, or being restrained or deflected by one person while trying to deal with a second?

What if you are wearing more restrictive clothing, for example, because you are wrapped up against the winter weather? It can be advisable to arrange a training session in which the effects of this are explored. This is not only because some techniques become far more difficult to perform (and also the clothing itself will provide some protection against certain attacks); it can also improve the awareness of, for example, being able to use a scarf as a flexible weapon.

The Characteristic of the Tool

It can be extremely important to make a quick judgement about the characteristics of any weapon wielded by your attacker. A blunt weapon may not cut, but it could shatter bone with immediate, intense pain. A club or an axe is likely to be used for large, open, strong, committed attacks, whereas a small knife could possibly be more dangerous, as it could be used deceptively and could not only slash and penetrate but also cut again on the way out or around limbs or previous targets.

If the attacker is outside physical contact range, it can obviously make an extremely significant difference if he is holding a gun rather than a club, as his weapon can damage you without him needing to get any closer. Your potential for disarming an attacker, or perhaps turning his own weapon against him, will depend on the nature of the weapon and the type of grip or hold he has on it.

If an attacker with an axe makes contact with your body, the likely effect is that you will be maimed or crippled, if not killed; whereas it may be possible to take a knife cut to a non-critical area (such as the back of your forearm) in the process of disarming him or neutralizing the attack. You may therefore need better avoidance and footwork skills against the large and dangerous weapon, but better close-range sensitivity skills against the smaller, bladed weapon.

It is often the case that engaging with an armed attacker is not the best strategy, and that if possible you would be advised to throw something into his face and make your escape. However, if he is holding a gun, and starts shooting, you may have done exactly the wrong thing. If there are other people in the vicinity, you will also need to take into consideration the angle of any attempt to deflect the weapon: if you are out walking with your elderly mother-in-law, it is hardly good strategy to push the weapon away from you and towards her, as you may easily make the situation far worse than it would have been!

The Principles of Training

Traditional training in the Philippines is based on individual coaching methods; this is because it is either taught on a one-to-one basis, or semi-privately in the form of a 'backyard' group. The Eskrima *Maestro* (Master) would teach only those techniques that he felt the student could make good use of. Thus, what he would teach to one student would differ in detail, or even in essence, from what was taught to another student. This is because it is situational – that is, the Maestro varies his technique depending upon the ability and physique of the student and the nature of the environment. Essentially, the student is taught to respond *appropriately* to any situation.

When operating a school or club, the training methods revolve around mass instruction and the *guro* (instructor) will use the 'whole-part-whole' approach to teaching: that is, the *whole* skill will be demonstrated to the students, and then it will be practised in parts. The whole skill will again be demonstrated, and the students will then practise it in its complete form.

The five stages for skill development in Warriors Eskrima are as follows:

1. **Learn:** The acquisition of fundamental motor skills.
2. **Practice:** Repetition, to integrate the skills into memory, muscle, balance and the nervous system.
3. **Master:** Perform the movements and techniques with 'correct form' to maximize their effectiveness.
4. **Functionalize:** Learn to apply them in practice, with appropriate speed and intensity, and against resistance or under pressure.
5. **Maintain:** Periodical review of the skills to ensure they remain functional.

3 *Solo Baston* – Single Stick

The single stick is perhaps the best known aspect of Eskrima. In fact, some practitioners refer to Eskrima as *baston*, or simply 'Filipino stick fighting'. However, the stick is a relatively modern development: originally the art was practised with long blades. But it was not until the Spanish banned the carrying of bladed weapons for tribal leaders that the natives took up the stick as a substitute.

Originally the sticks were flattened so as to resemble the shape of a long blade, and the sticks were made from hardwoods such as *kamagong* or *bahi*. These woods were ideal for duels or *juego todo* ('anything goes') challenge matches, popularly known as *bahad*.

However, for training purposes bahi or kamagong are unforgiving, and as a result rattan became the choice for the Eskrima stick. *Olisi* became a popular choice of rattan amongst many eskrimadors, as it is durable but not too dense; also the lighter weight compared to the hardwoods allowed for longer training sessions, and limited injuries to bruises as opposed to fractures.

Salutation (*Saludo*)

In every martial art there is a method of paying respects at the beginning and end of a training session: in some systems you bow, in

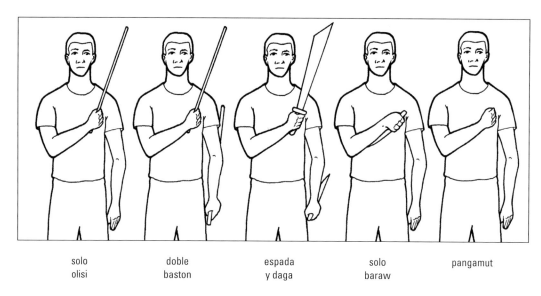

| solo olisi | doble baston | espada y daga | solo baraw | pangamut |

Salutation positions.

others you use different types of hand gestures. In the Filipino martial arts, the term *saludo*, meaning 'salute', is the command used for paying respects. The type of salutation can vary from system to system, varying from simple to complex. The method used in warriors' Eskrima is to stand with the feet shoulder-width apart, and when the teacher says '*saludo*', bring the right foot in so that it touches the left, at the same time bringing the right hand to the heart.

If you are holding a weapon in your left hand – for example, as in *doble baston* ('double stick') or *espada y daga* ('sword and dagger') – then this should be held in a reverse grip. The reverse grip should also be used when saluting with the *baraw* ('knife').

Normal hold.

Stick length measurement.

Weapon Length

The fundamentals of training with the single stick begin with understanding the optimal weapon length for each individual. To ascertain the ideal length, each individual should put one end of the stick into the armpit and stretch out their arm. Ideally, the stick should reach the middle finger.

Grips and Holds

Next the student should understand holds

Reverse hold.

Thumb extended grip.   Punch grip.   Thumb locked grip.

and grips; the actual manner of holding the stick will ultimately depend on personal preference and convenience. Of course, the style practised will also influence this choice. As students progress in their training, they will gain the feel, experience and insight as to the most efficient and effective way of holding the stick for themselves.

Irrespective of the style used, there are two basic ways of holding the stick, known as normal hold and reverse hold. Normal hold is where the long end of the stick is on the thumb portion of the hand holding it; reverse hold, as the name suggests, is when the long end of the stick is on the smallest finger portion of the hand holding the cane. This position often results from a successful disarming of the opponent's stick, and is a most versatile grip at close quarters.

The basic method of gripping the stick is to place it in the palm of your hand and simply wrap your fingers around it; however, be aware that there are four basic possibilities regarding the placement of your thumb. The first method is to place the thumb along the stick so that it is pointing towards the tip. This was the favoured grip of the older eskrimadors, and is very useful when using a sword because it adds direction to the cuts and makes them remarkably more severe and deep. It also helps increase the power of a thrusting attack, because the grip stops the wrist from bending. It is best used at *largo mano* (long range), which is the safest range when fighting with the long blade; however, if used at close quarters this grip can leave the eskrimador vulnerable to being disarmed.

Early practitioners of the art also placed a loop in their stick, where they inserted the middle finger. The main objective of this was to prevent the cane slipping from the hand. This method was quite popular when eskrimadors were using very heavy sticks. Today, many practitioners frown on this practice because of the risk of dislocation to the middle finger when the opponent uses disarming techniques.

The second method is to wrap the thumb around the index and middle fingers, as if making a fist to punch with. This is the most common grip, and is particularly effective at *corto* (close) range because it facilitates the *witik* or curved strikes. However, it is not the best grip when using a weighty sword because it is difficult to make a true cut with the edge, resulting in chopping strokes that, if they get home, inflict hardly more than superficial scratches.

The third method is to place the thumb over the middle finger and then wrap the index finger over it. Doing this makes it more difficult for your opponent to disarm you. It is the preferred grip for styles that are employed at medium and close range, where the risk of being disarmed by controlling the thumb is higher.

The fourth grip is the palm-assisted grip. This grip is used to gain extra reach when delivering a thrust; it also tremendously increases the power of the thrust, as the stick is 'power-assisted' by the palm of the hand. The limitation of this grip is that you can deliver only thrusting strikes; therefore, it is generally employed as a transitory grip.

Next there is the issue of where exactly to position the hand when holding the stick. Some styles have an allowance of 2in (5cm) at the bottom of the stick; this can vary up to an allowance of 6in. This butt portion of the stick is called the *punyo* or *pokpok*. Conversely, some systems advocate having no allowance for a *punyo* – so let us look at the advantages and disadvantages of each method.

The short *punyo* – up to 2in (5cm) – is the preferred grip for close range stylists; at this range the *punyo* serves various purposes. It can be used effectively for striking – especially for setting up the various curved strikes; it also allows the eskrimador to execute a number of disarms, and can also set up a number of locks and throws.

The long *punyo* – 4 to 6in (10 to 15cm) – is usually preferred by eskrimadors who participate in tournaments. This is because the stick, which is gripped by a gloved hand (worn for protection), tends to slip during the duration of the bout – so this grip is advocated so as to not disarm oneself.

On one of my early trips to the Philippines, while training with Grandmaster Fortunato 'Atong' Garcia, I noticed that he used the long *punyo*, which enabled him to change holds, or transfer the stick from the right hand to the left, very efficiently. So this is another advantage of such a hold. However, a disadvantage of this grip is that it reduces one's reach considerably and so gives the opponent the opportunity to divest you of the stick by grabbing the *punyo*.

The styles that use no *punyo* give several reasons for it. First, by holding the stick at the base, you maximize your reach. This is a

Palm-assisted grip.

Long punyo grip.

Largo mano grip.

preferred grip for *largo mano* stylists, who have no intention of closing, and hence no use for the *punyo*. Their principal method of disarming their opponent is to hit his weapon hand with long-range strikes such as slashes, as opposed to the close-range stylist who likes to use the *punyo* to strike or 'eject' his opponent's stick when attempting to disarm him.

The limitations of not having a *punyo* are that you have taken away one of your close-range weapons, and it is not safe to assume that you can always keep your opponent from closing. Second, if you do not have a good grip you run the risk of your weapon slipping out of your hand.

This brings us to the issue of gripping effectively. The grip is a fundamental and highly important aspect in the practice of Eskrima. It must be firm, not too tight nor too loose. Too tight a grip restricts wrist movement and reduces speed and power; too loose a grip and you run the risk of disarming oneself. The optimal pressure one should apply is something one learns through experience and long practice.

The secret for generating speed, power and force as well as control is the grip. According to Grandmaster Abner Pasa:

> The proper way of gripping the stick is to use the middle and ring finger to securely hold the stick, whilst the forefinger and index finger are used for control purposes. The thumb serves as a lock and provides additional control when executing the witik. The grip should be light and flexible. The wrist should remain flexible so that the hand can rotate as one swings the stick.
>
> When executing full extension thrusting techniques, use only three fingers: the thumb, middle finger and ring finger. Holding the stick with all five fingers is disadvantageous, especially when you thrust forwards at full extension, because it will be difficult to hold the cane straight, resulting in a weak strike due to excessive bend in the wrist. This action weakens your wrist, and could cause damage in actual combat.

When delivering curved strikes the index finger and the small finger serve to check the momentum of the cane, while the thumb acts as a lock. To focus the power of the blows, you must tense and tighten the grip at the moment of impact. This action adds momentum to the strike and increases acceleration of the stick. It also allows the force to be completely focused at point of impact. The practice of gripping the stick very tightly on impact also prevents the accidental slippage of the stick from the hand.

Stance

The stance in Eskrima is very similar to a boxing stance. The toes of the lead leg are slightly turned in, and the rear heel is raised. To get the correct width, walk a couple of paces forward, and stop. The correct stance should facilitate balance, mobility and stability.

On Guard Postures

There are many on guard postures in Eskrima. Some postures are used as a

Basic stance.

Abierta posture.

Serada posture.

Tutsada posture.

platform to deliver specific strikes, others are used for defensive manoeuvres, and yet others are used for 'drawing' – exposing a false opening to draw the opponents attack. The three basic on guard postures used in Eskrima are *abierta* (open), *serada* (closed) and *tutsada* (thrust).

The *abierta* posture can be used to deliver powerful strikes, such as the forehand slash, or it can be used for 'tip up' blocking.

The *serada* posture can be used to deliver backhand slashes, and it also lends itself well for parrying strikes.

The *tutsada* posture is used to deliver a thrusting motion with the stick; the thrust can be both a strike or, if hooked, will work as a parry.

Footwork

Since the Filipino martial arts are weapons-based systems, footwork is critical, and you have to move in order to avoid being hit. However, due to the extra reach a weapon gives, much of the footwork involves 'switching' leads; staying constantly in the same lead does not get you out of striking distance against weapon attacks.

Forward triangle (left lead).

Intermediate position.

Forward triangle (right lead).

Backward triangle (left lead).

Intermediate position.

Backward triangle (right lead).

I teach seven basic footwork patterns: the first is the forward triangle, whose purpose is to teach switching leads in a forward direction; it is excellent for coordination as both legs are evenly used. Note that the lead leg moves first when performing this pattern.

The second pattern is the backward triangle, which teaches the ability to switch leads in a backward direction; it is also excellent for coordination, as both legs are evenly used. Note that the rear leg moves first when executing this movement pattern.

The third pattern is called the side triangle (advance), and involves moving the rear leg forwards, in the process 'shifting' leads. Note that the lead leg does not move.

The fourth pattern is exactly the same movement in the opposite direction; the side triangle (retreat) is performed by moving the lead leg backwards. Note that the rear leg does not move. When you combine strikes with this type of footwork it is called 'switch hitting'.

The fifth footwork pattern is the pivot, and as the name suggests, you pivot with the rear leg; the objective is to avoid a straight attack to your torso's abdomen. The

Side triangle (left lead).

Advance.

Side triangle (left lead).

Retreat.

Ready stance.

Pivot.

Ready stance.   Push forward.   Push back.

advantage of this pattern is that it often allows you to counter from outside the opponent's line of vision.

The sixth pattern is called the push forwards; there is no switching of leads in this pattern. The rear leg acts as the power driver, whilst the lead leg is the range finder. It needs to be an explosive movement, and one way to develop this explosive feel is to have a partner push you forwards towards a wall. After doing the required number of repetitions, do the movement without your training partner's assistance and you will automatically get the kinetic feeling of advancing explosively.

The seventh and final pattern is called the push back, where the lead leg acts as the power driver to push you in a backward direction. You can use the wall to assist you with the motion, but have a training partner to support you from the back, should you lose your balance. The use of the wall will help you with the explosive movement required to retreat rapidly.

The Targeting System

Once the student has been introduced to the various holds and grips, also to stance, on guard postures and basic footwork, the next progression is to introduce a targeting system. This will consist of a combination of different strikes, which can be classified into four basic types:

1. Slash – a movement that follows through from one side of the body to the other.
2. Thrust – a thrusting attack with the tip of the stick; it can be delivered in a linear or hooking motion.
3. *Witik* – a wrist-orientated strike; it includes fanning motions (*abaniko*), and curving or snapping strikes.
4. *Punyo* – a strike with the handle or butt of the stick; *punyo* strikes can be rakes or hammerfist motions.

If you are learning a traditional system of Eskrima, Kali or Arnis, regardless of which part of the Philippines it originates in, it will include lessons in various angles of attack, often called *numerada*. This training method was developed so as to familiarize the eskrimador with the various angles of attack, instead of confusing the student by naming each strike – a simple system of 'referral by number' was adopted.

According to the late Grandmaster

Slash strike.

Witik strike.

Thrust strike.

Punyo strike.

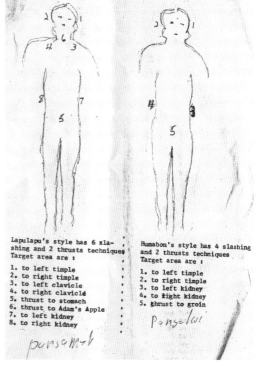

Lapulapu's style has 6 slashing and 2 thrusts techniques Target area are :

1. to left timple
2. to right timple
3. to left clavicle
4. to right clavicle
5. thrust to stomach
6. thrust to Adam's Apple
7. to left kidney
8. to right kidney

punsamah

Humabon's style has 4 slashing and 2 thrusts techniques Target area are :

1. to left timple
2. to right timple
3. to left kidney
4. to right kidney
5. thrust to groin

Ponselari

Eulogio Canete – *numerada* archives.

Numerada template.

WARRIORS ESKRIMA
Single Stick Numerada

1. Diagonal downward slash to the left temple

2. Diagonal downward slash to right knee

3. Horizontal strike to left elbow

4. Downward slash to right temple

5. Palm down thrust to the navel

6. Upward slash to right upper ribcage

7. Upward slash to left upper ribcage

8. Palm up thrust to throat

9. Palm down thrust to heart

10. Palm up thrust to right lung

11. Hooking thrust to left eye

12. Hooking thrust to right eye

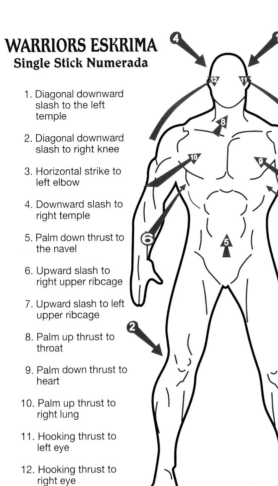

SOLO BASTON

Angle 1.

Angle 2.

Angle 3.

Angle 4.

Angle 5.

Angle 6.

Angle 7.

Angle 8.

Angle 9.

Angle 10.

Angle 11.

Angle 12.

Eulogio 'Ingko Yoling' Canete, the angles of attack can be traced back to the time of the great Lapu Lapu, whose style used six slashing and two thrusting techniques, while Datu Humabon's style taught four slashes and one thrust. Over time, the more modern styles of Eskrima increased the numbering system to ten, and eventually twelve angles. Today you can find styles that teach up to sixty-four angles of attack.

Some masters believe that the original aim of having a numbering system was to offer a simple training method that familiarized the student with various targets on the body, and that by giving a number to each particular angle it would be easier to remember, as opposed to giving each strike a 'different name', especially with so many different dialects in the Philippines.

Another method that was taught to the eskrimador was known as the 'star' pattern. This method taught the student angle/line familiarization, not by numbers but by lines. A combination of diagonal, horizontal and vertical lines was used: the student would practise slashing techniques following these lines, and thrusting techniques to various points on the pattern.

Another method that was also taught was similar to that of Western fencing. Known as the quadrant system, the body was basically split horizontally and vertically, thereby presenting a high/low and left/right quadrant. Some eskrimadors preferred this method, as it is the simplest approach and can be adapted to any style, whereas the numbering system always differs from style to style.

The following numbering system is from Grandmaster Vicente Carin's Eskrima system.

Numerada gives the student a base structure from which the *abecedario* can be practised. *Abecedario* refers to the 'abc' of the art: typically this would cover defensive skills, counter-striking, disarming, off-balancing and immobilizing.

Traditionally, the ability not to get hit is highly regarded in Eskrima: this is because everyone can pick up a stick and strike with it, but effective defence is less natural and requires more training. In the past, at fiestas throughout the Philippines, eskrimadors would stand on three coconut shells and ask children to try and hit them with a stick. The eskrimador would evade the strikes by using triangle footwork, or by blocking, parrying or deflecting the strikes with their own stick. The eskrimador would lose if he lost his balance and came off the shells, or if he was hit – but he rarely lost.

The first stage of developing defensive skills is to block single direct attacks. One person feeds the *numerada*, and the other person blocks. Once the basic mechanics of blocking are learned, the feeder can hit harder to ensure that grip, hand alignment and structure of the technique is solid. Once this is established, the next stage would be to fine tune the blocks so that they are tight and efficient. Two methods are used to develop this: the first is to attack with a progressive indirect attack – this involves faking (called *lansi*, *enganyo* or *huwad*). If the student's blocks are too exaggerated then he will be hit, because as he tries to reach out to block one strike, the feeder will have faked and changed the line of attack.

The other method is to feed the *numerada* with two sticks. Since the person blocking will be restricted to one stick, his blocks will have to be tight in order to deal with both sticks; in essence when defending one should endeavour to 'hide behind the stick'. For illustrative purposes, the blocking method exhibited follows the methodology that all strikes above the chest are blocked with the tip of the stick facing *up*, while all strikes delivered below the chest are blocked with the tip of the stick facing *down*.

Angle 1: Tip-up block.

Angle 2: Tip-down block.

Angle 3: Tip-down block.

Angle 4: Tip-up block.

Angle 5: Tip-down parry.

Angle 6: Tip-down block.

Angle 7: Tip-down block.

Angle 8: Tip-up block.

Angle 9: Tip-up block.

Angle 10: Tip-up block.

Angle 11: Tip-up block.

Angle 12: Tip-up block.

Once competency in meeting the force of the strike (blocking) is achieved, the next stage is to develop the ability to follow the force of the strike, which involves parrying and deflecting. These skills are taught after blocking because they require better timing to execute successfully. They are also the preferred method of defence when using a sword, as blocking could damage the cutting edge of the blade.

Once proficiency in blocking, parrying and deflecting are achieved, the next stage is to bring into play the secondary hand, also known as the 'live hand' or *bantay kamay*. In many classical styles of Eskrima, the live hand is developed through the *espada y daga* or *olisi y baraw* training. By putting a *daga* or knife in the secondary hand (left hand for most practitioners) it becomes more active – hence the term 'alive' or 'live' hand.

The *bantay kamay* can be used for checking, disarming, locking or striking. When checking the opponent's weapon, the palm of the hand and fingers are used to control and off-set the opponent's attacking options, while at the same time one takes advantage of the opportunity to counter attack with one's own stick.

The following rare illustration is from a book called *Destreza Del Espadin* (1805), written by Manuel Antonio de Brea. Note the *ritirada* step, the use of the live hand, and counter with the *punyo*.

The following two rare photos show excellent use of the live hand, demonstrated by the graceful Grandmaster Frederico Serfino.

LEFT: Spanish Esgrima – Manuel Brea (1805).

BELOW: Parry and simultaneous strike (Serfino Arnis).

Block and simultaneous elbow check (Serfino Arnis).

BELOW: *Amara* figures (numbers 1–6).

The *Amara*

Counter attacks are often grouped under *contras*, or *amara*. The *contras* can consist of various 'styles' or 'methods', such as *herada*, *ritirada*, *redonda* and so on. The *amara* consists of a wide variety of strikes, including linear strikes, circular strikes, thrusts, figure-eight strikes. The progression should be to start with simple counter strikes, and then move to more complex combinations.

The figures illustrated are an easy way to learn the *amara*, though due to space limitations, only the first three sequences are shown. Imagine that the tip of your stick is a pen, and that you are following the arrow lines.

The following sequences show how to practise the *amara* on striking pads: using pads helps to develop accuracy and power. Due to space limitations, only *amaras* 1 to 3 are shown in their entirety, plus the unique strikes contained in *amaras* 5 and 6.

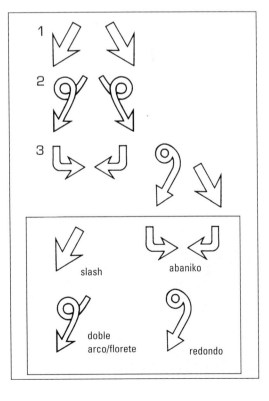

Amara No. 1

ABOVE: Forehand slash (*Amara* 1).

TOP LEFT: On-guard position (*Amara* 1).

LEFT: Backhand slash (*Amara* 1).

Amara No. 2

On-guard position
(*Amara* 2).

Forehand slash
(*Amara* 2).

Intermediate position
(*Amara* 2).

Forehand slash (*Amara* 2).

Backhand slash (*Amara* 2).

Intermediate position (*Amara* 2).

Backhand slash (*Amara* 2).

Amara No. 3

On-guard position
(*Amara* 3).

Forehand *abaniko*
(*Amara* 3).

Backhand *abaniko*
(*Amara* 3).

Redondo strike (*Amara* 3).

Backhand slash (*Amara* 3).

Amara No. 5

The uppercut strike in *Amara* No. 5 is exhibited below:

Uppercut strike (*Amara* 5).

Amara No. 6

The 'low' *abaniko* strike used in *Amara* No. 6 is exhibited below:

Disarming

Once checking and counter-attacking skills have been developed, disarming manoeuvres (called *agaw*) would be the next skill set to develop. The ability to disarm an opponent is a highly regarded skill, as it is more difficult to effect than striking. There are many disarming manoeuvres available to the eskrimador, but different ones are more effective at different ranges. At long range (*larga mano*) the most effective disarming technique is to strike the hand holding your opponent's weapon, or if he is holding the stick loosely, then a percussion strike to his stick will result in him being disarmed.

At medium range (*medio mano*), the *bantay kamay* can come into play by either grabbing the opponent's stick, or binding it with a 'snaking' movement. The most common disarming manoeuvres in this range are therefore 'grab' or 'snake' manoeuvres.

ABOVE: Hand smash disarming manoeuvre.

MIDDLE LEFT: Low forehand *abaniko* (*Amara* 6).

LEFT: Low backhand *abaniko* (*Amara* 6).

Grab and fulcrum disarming manoeuvre.

Punyo grab disarming manoeuvre.

Snake disarming manoeuvre.

Punyo stripping disarming manoeuvre.

Punyo lever disarming manoeuvre.

At close range (*dikit* or *corto mano*), the most effective disarming techniques are those effected with the *punyo*. Commonly called 'stripping', 'quick release' or 'ejecting', the mechanics of this type of disarming manoeuvre revolve around the live hand controlling the opponent's thumb. The thumb is the lock in terms of the opponent retaining a secure grip on his weapon, so if the lock is 'opened' by peeling the thumb open, then the weapon can be dislodged. Also, note that the opponent's wrist is also 'locked' when applying this type of disarming manoeuvre; locking the wrist puts the hand in a weak position and hence negates the opponent's ability to retain his weapon.

The final types of disarming moves available at close range are those which involve using the opponent's *punyo* against himself. For example, you can grab the opponent's *punyo* and dislodge it, or you could grab the opponent's wrist and lever against their *punyo*.

Takedowns

The final basic skill set to develop would be grappling techniques such as locking, chokes/strangles and takedowns. All of these three areas are interchangeable, and should flow from one to the other. For example, as the opponent attempts to get out of a lock, he leaves himself open for a choke or takedown.

There are numerous ways of using the stick to off-balance your opponent; one way to remember all the off-balancing points on the body is to use the 'clock system'. This method is based on a clockwise sequence of takedowns working around the opponent's body, starting from the wrist, and moving to elbow, armpit, shoulders, ribcage and legs.

The following illustration highlights the different points on the body, where a stick can be used to off-balance an opponent.

The following photographs exhibit the basic eight takedown positions:

ABOVE: Takedown number 1.

LEFT: Stick takedowns – clock system diagram

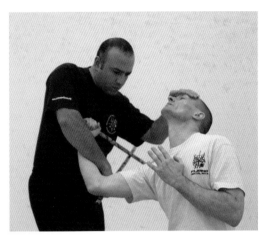

Takedown number 2.

Takedown number 3.

Takedown number 4.

Takedown number 5.

Takedown number 6.

Takedown number 7.

Takedown number 8.

Locks

Locking with the stick involves attacking various joints on the body. These include the wrist, elbow, shoulder, knee and ankle. According to Guro Dan Inosanto:

> A lock occurs when the opponent is immobilized by placing a fulcrum across one of his joints, causing pressure in a direction that the joint isn't intended to bend, preferably where the joint is weakest.
>
> The fulcrum of a lock is made up with a triangle. The first side is a part of the opponent's arm that is between the joint you plan to work on and his body, making it the stable side of your lock. The second side is the movable part of the opponent's arm. This side could be the entire arm (for shoulder locks), the lower arm (for elbow locks) or just the hand (for wrist locks). It is the side that will be manipulated against the natural function of the joint. You are the third side. By forming a link with your hand or forearm or both, you pry the movable part of the opponent's arm against the stable part. The stable side of the triangle is where the point of the fulcrum is located.
>
> Bent arm locks bend the joint sideways, while straight arm locks bend the joint exactly opposite its natural bend. With a straight arm lock, both ends of the opponent's arm become fairly stable while pressure is applied to the joint in the middle.

The following photo shows an example of a wrist lock, called the 'S' lock, as the opponent's arm looks like the letter S.

The following photo shows a very painful elbow lock, in which the tricep tendon is attacked to ensure the opponent fully cooperates:

Wrist lock.

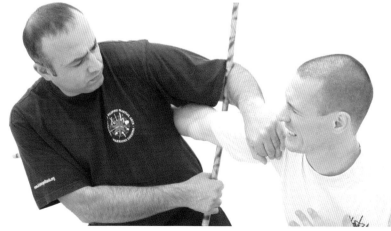

Elbow lock.

The following sequence shows how to close the gap and obtain a shoulder lock:

On-guard position.

Block and grab opponent's stick.

Manipulate opponent's stick behind arm, simultaneously strike temple.

Hook opponent's stick with your *punyo*.

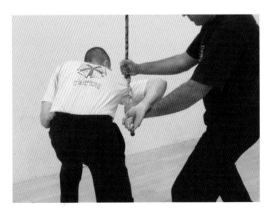

Pull opponent's stick down.

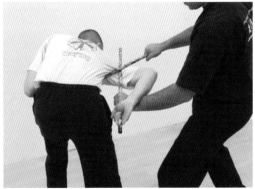

Insert stick into armpit and apply shoulder lock.

Flow Drills

Once a student develops a strong foundation using the *numerada* as the training framework, he or she can move on to flow drills. Flow can be defined as continuity of movement. In order to flow effectively, a combination of awareness and sensitivity is needed, which is achieved via uninterrupted concentration. The Filipino eskrimadors are famous for their ability to flow smoothly, and one of the ways this ability is developed is through the use of training drills known as 'flow drills'.

Different martial arts have different methods of developing required skills. One of the difficulties often faced by instructors is the difference between a structured, predictable series of movements, perhaps in an organized pattern or drill, or as a 'self-defence technique', and the apparent chaos of freestyle sparring. If there is no intermediate form of activity, then the student gets lost in the transition and cannot see the connection between structured training techniques and real-world fighting ability. It is like trying to teach him to swim by taking him from the paddling pool and throwing him in at the deep end, when, wildly floundering, he will fail to see any connection between 'real swimming' and the previous ways of being taught how to move and control his or her body in the water in the security of the 'shallow end'.

As students are acquiring and developing fundamental abilities, they need a form of training activity that overcomes this difficulty. As long as they are used properly, the flow drills of Filipino martial arts accomplish this with a high level of intelligence and technical proficiency. In the earliest stages a flow drill will indeed be a deliberate, structured and predictable series of movements. Each training partner will alternate an attack and a defence, with normally any number from three to seven movements in a repeated cycle. This is already a higher level of skill

acquisition than simply doing a number of stop-start repetitions of a single technique, as it already requires flow, reactions, accuracy in dealing with a variety of positions and targets, and judgment of timing and distance, depending on your training partner's movements. The student is therefore not only acquiring 'flow', but also developing other attributes, including coordination, reaction speed and sensitivity.

To maintain the flow, you have to continuously counter the opponent's attack, which is why flow drills are sometimes referred to by the terms *sombrada* (to shadow) or *contra y contra* (counter for counter). Flow drills can be performed with any weapon or with empty hands.

When the flow of movements in the fundamental drill has been acquired by the 'muscle memory', then the instructor can gradually introduce variables. At different points in a particular flow drill it may be possible to change the type of attack, or the target or level – for example, a low strike is substituted for a high strike.

What this means is that the student will initially have a fundamentally structured drill, but at one point in this drill he will not know which of two possible movements his training partner will use. He will be forced to come out of the 'robotic' flow of a permanently predictable drill, and acquire the flexibility to react in an 'appropriate' way at the last moment. Clearly this is a relatively safe way of increasing variability of defensive reactions, because at this stage the drill does not 'deteriorate' into free sparring.

It may then be appropriate for variable movements to be introduced at two stages of the drill, instead of just one. In this way, instead of having the conflict of 'structured training versus freestyle sparring', there can actually be a more or less continuous spectrum of training activity, with the safest and steadiest basic flow drill at one end, then the gradual introduction of different variables, through to free sparring at the other end.

(The variables can be more subtle than changing a low attack to a high attack, as the senior of the training partners can also deliberately use variability in the rhythm of movements, rather than simply repeating attacks 'on the beat' in a one-and-two-and-three, and so forth, drill.)

The student is therefore able to use flow drills to acquire the appropriate reactions, flexibility and flow, at their own pace, and this effectively merges into far more flexible give-and-take sparring, which has much more to do with the spontaneity of sparring than with the predictability of a training routine.

The following flow drill is called *sinko-sinko*: originally developed for a sword, it is a long-range five-count drill that teaches how to thrust, deflect and parry.

Deflect opponent's abdominal thrust.

Counter with palm-up thrust.

Opponent defends with tip-down deflection.

Opponent counters with palm-up thrust.

Defend with counter-clockwise parry.

Counter with palm-down thrust to eye.

Opponent defends with tip-up parry.

Parry opponent's eye thrust.

Repeat drill vice versa.

The next drill is called *higut hubad/ palakaw* defence; its aim is to teach one person how to use the 'live hand' for lifting, clearing and trapping, while the other person learns how to block with the stick at close range.

Sparring Drills

Once a student can develop the ability to flow with the stick, he would be ready to progress to sparring drills. Sparring drills with the stick start to develop timing, distance appreciation and footwork. The key

On-guard position.

Opponent blocks your forehand *punyo* strike.

Opponent establishes forearm-to-forearm contact.

Opponent traps your elbow.

Counter by grabbing your opponent's wrist, and lift their arm up.

Opponent defends your leg strike with a downward block.

Maintain wrist grab and slash to temple, which opponent blocks.

Release the wrist grab and check your opponent's stick hand.

Opponent blocks your backhand *punyo* strike.

Trap your opponent's arms and deliver backhand slash to the head: opponent blocks.

Clear opponent's stick arm down.

Repeat drill.

towards developing sparring is to theme it. The first stage would be to limit all strikes to the arms only, as this isolates the ability to hit and avoid strikes to the arms in long range sparring.

The following drill is called the 'U-hand defence drill', and its purpose is to teach you how to evade your opponent's hand strikes; the evasive technique makes a 'U' shape, hence the name.

On-guard position.

Opponent attempts a hand smash.

Evade by dipping under your opponent's stick in a clockwise direction.

Evasion completed.

Counter with a hand smash.

The next drill is called the 'Half X hand defence drill'. It teaches you how to block your opponent's strike, with 'half' of an X motion. This type of defence lends itself perfectly to counter with a thrust.

One very useful exercise I learned from Grandmaster Romy Macapagal (the Kalis Ilustrisimo system) is to put something under your armpit while practising your strikes. If the object falls to the floor, it means that you are leading with your hand and thus exposing your arm to counter strikes. By keeping the armpit tight you learn to strike with the 'tip' of your weapon.

On-guard position.

Opponent attempts a hand smash: block by pulling *punyo* towards your hip.

Counter with an eye thrust.

Striking without dropping the object held under the armpit.

The next target to include would be the legs. Because of the extended reach possible with the stick, the footwork required to avoid the strikes has to cover extra distance; merely straightening the leg or shuffling back will not often avoid the strike. I teach two basic movements to avoid leg strikes: the cross step, and the rear shift of lead. Note how the footwork avoids the strike, while your stick remains in range to counter attack to the head.

As one moves from long range to medium and close range, additional targets come within reach, namely the torso and head.

Your opponent attempts a leg strike.

Evade with a cross step, and a simultaneous strike to the temple.

Evade with a *ritirada* step and a simultaneous strike to the forehead.

The torso is usually targeted with thrusts and slashes, and the defences for these are as taught in the *numerada*.

The head is a major target: when engaged in combat with blunt impact weapons – such as sticks – the altercation is most likely to end when a strike is delivered to the temple or occipital, as this would render the individual unconscious. This is unlike combat with bladed weapons, when a much wider variety of targets can end the conflict. It is therefore crucial to develop sound defensive skills to protect the head. Two simple yet highly effective defences to the head are the roof block, and the reverse roof block. Note how the block can be 'reinforced': this is crucial when blocking very powerful strikes.

Sparring drills allow you to isolate targets and role play. This takes away the chaos of sparring, and eases the student in; it assures more skill development by allowing the student to develop confidence in the techniques.

Once the student has developed repertoire and good form, he is ready for freestyle sparring. Freestyle sparring can come in many forms; this can be controlled (non contact) or it can be full contact. Controlled freestyle sparring is called *palakaw*, where techniques are delivered at full speed but pulled before contact is made. Full contact sparring can be done with armour using rattan sticks, or without armour using padded sticks; all of these types of sparring have their advantages and disadvantages.

Reinforced roof block.

Reverse roof block.

Full contact sparring with full body armour offers more protection (fewer injuries) to the eskrimadors, but can hinder movement and vision. Full contact sparring without armour eliminates these hindrances, but can increase the chances of injury, especially if the students do not have sound defensive skills. *Palakaw* is the safest form of sparring, yet it is like a chess match and requires a very high level of proficiency in Eskrima to perform effectively; this explains why it is so popular amongst many Masters and Grandmasters.

Author and GM Pasa playing *palakaw*.

Full-contact sparring with padded sticks and fencing helmets.

GM Pasa and Master Berdin playing *palakaw*.

Full-contact sparring with full body armour and rattan sticks.

4 *Baraw* – Knife Defence

Many edged-weapons authorities regard the Filipino martial arts (Eskrima, Kali, Arnis) to be among the most practical systems for edged-weapons defence. They are used to train not just civilians but law enforcement personnel, security professionals and various Special Forces around the world. Since this book is primarily aimed at the civilian market, techniques relating to 'knife fighting' have been omitted, and the focus of this chapter is on self-defence against knife attacks.

Being threatened by someone with a knife is, to many people, the most frightening form of threat that could be faced – and this is not necessarily because of any conscious awareness that more people actually survive gunshot wounds than knife attacks. A bullet may very well be more dangerous than a knife, but most people do not have the experience of having been shot, while virtually everyone has suffered an accidental cut at some time – so the idea of what the knife can do to you is psychologically more 'real'.

As news reports unfortunately demonstrate, even in the hands of a young and completely untrained individual, a knife is potentially lethal. The characteristics of the weapon make it extremely dangerous, as it may open blood vessels or tear supporting tendons or muscles with a slashing movement, or it can easily penetrate vital organs with a thrusting movement. It is therefore important to appreciate that if you 'freeze up', this can only make you incapable of effective movement or defensive tactics. If you are to have any hope of dealing with such a deadly weapon, you need to acquire the right mindset and the appropriate set of skills.

Awareness

The first skill to develop would be awareness, because good awareness may give you the option to avoid the conflict altogether, or to control it in its earliest stages.

This awareness principle was firmly ingrained in my mind when I saw a stabbing in Cebu City, the Philippines. I was staying in a rather cheap hotel located outside the tourist belt; on the opposite side of the road was a shanty bar. I noticed two men arguing, whilst a third manoeuvred behind one of them. This third guy then grabbed the man's arms from behind, while the other took out a knife and proceeded to deliver multiple stabs. 'Tunnel vision' – lack of awareness of what was happening near him – may have cost this person his life.

If possible, the best response is always to escape. If you can possibly avoid an altercation by running or walking away, you must take it, and never give in to any impulse to express your anger or 'get involved' in something that is avoidable simply by going away. Unfortunately, this option may not always be available. Perhaps the exit route is between you and the attacker. Perhaps you have loved ones to protect, or running away would mean deserting an innocent victim who is likely to have no martial arts' knowledge or ability. In such cases your best strategy is some kind of 'equalizer' – anything that you can lay your hands on in the vicinity which can be used as a projectile, shield, flexible weapon or impact weapon.

A projectile could be something you are carrying or that you can pick up and throw at the attacker, such as coins or keys or pens. This may very well create the opportunity for your escape, or if necessary for you to deliver a strike or to pick up another 'equalizer'. A shield could be a 'close' shield, such as having a jacket or shoe over your arm or in the hand, or something that you can pick up or move around so that it is between you and the attacker. A flexible weapon could be something like a scarf or a belt, something that can be flicked out sharply.

The following is a real-life example of an eskrimador in the Philippines using an available implement and a flexible weapon to defend himself against three attackers. Borg, a Badjao Muslim warrior from Jolo, was attacked on Osmena Boulevard in Cebu City. He was hit on the head with a beer bottle, and staggered into a food vendor's stand. The attackers came in after him. First he grabbed a pork skewer from the stand, and used it to keep them at bay. This gave him the opportunity to remove his belt, which had a huge brass buckle. He then used this as a whip to prevent his attackers from closing in, and was able to escape safely.

Awareness also includes the following:

- that there may be a weapon, even though you may not yet have seen it, which is yet to be drawn;
- that you need to consider body language and postures, because these will provide clues as to whether a knife is being carried;
- that in a threatening situation, you cannot jump to conclusions about the psychology or motivation of your attacker.

During the dialogue that often precedes an altercation, the opponent may be considering whether or not he wants to access his weapon. You need to try and maintain good peripheral awareness, so that you can notice any attempt on his part to draw the weapon. The adrenalin of fear can be useful if it is providing you with energy to fight or escape, but it is usually accompanied by 'tunnel vision'.

It is better to try and stay calm enough to be aware of what he is or may be doing, rather than becoming drawn into being 'obsessed' with the face of an angry person in front of you. You need to try and de-personalize the situation to reduce the emotional content of it, imagining him objectively as lines of attack and potential targets, instead of as something 'frightening'. You will never be as calm and confident as you would like to be in such a situation, but any deliberate reduction in your own tension will also prevent your own verbal or physical reactions from making a situation worse.

A knife can be holstered in many positions: in the belt or the pocket seem fairly obvious, but a knife can also be carried at the chest or behind the neck, or at the ankle. Certain postures allow for quick drawing and deployment of the blade, and it is crucial to recognize these postures so that you can:

- stop the knife from being deployed by trapping the opponent's arms or hand;
- deliver a pre-emptive strike as he reaches for it;
- be ready at least to try and deal with it if you are not close enough or fast enough to prevent the weapon being drawn.

Without awareness, these strategies are impossible. Not realizing that there was a knife in the situation, a number of people have only discovered after a 'fight', or an apparently unarmed attack, that they have been cut or stabbed (because of detecting bleeding).

Hidden blade – reverse grip.

Hidden blade – forward grip.

Blade carried in the pants.

Hand position used to conceal a blade.

It can be seen that there may be a number of stages prior to engaging with a knife. If you cultivate good awareness you increase your chances of utilizing these options. However, the attacker may already be showing a knife, or you may be taken by surprise. It is then vital not to assume that you can simply avoid harm by 'doing what he says' or 'giving him what he wants', and that 'he will then go away'. This is a foolish and potentially suicidal assumption. You are in danger, and you may stay in danger until you *know*

the threat has been neutralized – not only until you have handed over your wallet.

You do not know this person. You do not know what substances they may have taken, or what psychological background they have. They may be desperate for money; they may be inveterate liars; they may say one thing and mean another. They may say they want your credit cards, when what they really want is to distract you into thinking this is a robbery, and what they really want is a victim to hurt. They may rob you, and *then* decide to hurt you, for 'kicks'.

They might have a peculiar need to humiliate or dominate a victim, followed by which they may decide that you could identify them, and they really don't want to go to jail. You might have given them what you thought they needed, but then they decide they cannot afford to leave you alive as a witness, so even though you have handed over your credit cards and your wristwatch, you are *still* going to have to defend yourself against a knife attack.

It *may* be the case that the person wants to rob you, and that if you give him what he asks for, he will go away. So give him what he asks for. It doesn't matter what it is: it matters that you survive. But don't then think 'Oh, thank God, I've given him my money' and then mentally collapse because it is 'almost over'. Keep your mind in a state of high alertness, ready to move and ready to use your Eskrima skills if he still decides he is going to attack you. You may be lucky: he may go away. But if he is not going to go away, it is only your maintained awareness, and then your training in self-defence, that will increase the statistical chances of your survival.

One very useful tactic to remember is to shout '*knife!*' loudly the moment you see the weapon; this can catch the attention of others nearby, and means that the knife is no longer a weapon of 'stealth' for the attacker. Psychologically this can 'turn the tables' and may make the attacker flee.

Grips, Attacks and Targets

In training, it is necessary to look at what the attacker may do to you. Training with a

Forward/hammer grip.

Thumb-supported grip.

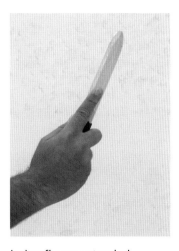

Index finger extended grip.

Extended thumb and index grip.

Reverse/ice-pick grip.

Punyo-supported grip.

wooden or aluminium knife has nothing to do with 'encouraging' the carrying of knives. Carrying a knife (other than because of certain professional or religious reasons) is almost invariably illegal in the UK. Carrying a knife for 'self-defence' reasons is extremely dangerous, because in a heated argument there is a temptation to draw it. In an encounter that would otherwise not have involved any weapons, it is perfectly possible for the knife to be taken from you, whether deliberately or accidentally, and used against you. Your 'self-defence' could then result in your own death. Such a reason for carrying a knife is therefore very dangerous and never justifiable.

Slash.

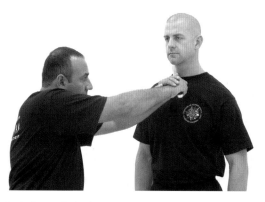

Reinforced slash.

Palm up thrust.

Power-assisted thrust.

Forehand stab (reverse grip).

Training with knives – that is, non-edged and non-pointed training weapons only – is absolutely necessary to develop any useful understanding of how to defend yourself against them. If you can see the knife – that is, it has already been drawn – then it will be held in either a forward grip, also known as a hammer grip, or in a reverse grip, also known as the ice-pick grip. The reverse grip is more favoured for concealment, but the forward grip has a longer reach. The photos are examples of various knife grips.

The two most common types of attack with a knife are thrusts and slashes. Typically, thrusts are more serious because of the depth of penetration into the body, which may result in damage to vital organs and internal bleeding. The effect of slashes can often be reduced by such factors as layers of clothing. The following are examples of basic slash and thrust attacks.

A certain awareness of anatomy will influence defensive strategies against the knife. Clearly it is vital to try and prevent cuts to the neck and throat, where there is danger to the carotid arteries and the breathing system. There is substantial risk from a cut to arteries on the arm (such as the brachial artery, on the inside of the arm under the biceps), or the femoral artery, running down the inner thigh from the middle of the hip crease. However, more than half of knife wounds are to the abdominal or chest area, and the dangers here are enormous because of possible injury to stomach and intestines, lungs and heart, liver and kidneys. Thrusts into the back will also endanger the heart and lungs as well as the spinal cord and the major abdominal aorta artery, which runs down close to the spine before branching into the iliac arteries, which feed blood to the hip area and then the legs.

Note: For a detailed explanation of anatomy and its practical implications for knife defence (*see* Understanding Anatomy, p. 164).

Untrained people trying to defend against a knife attacker will often hold up their hands in front of their face, and may acquire 'defensive wounds' across the open hands and the inside of the arms. This is a good example of a reflexive reaction, which is not the most appropriate response – it increases the risk of a cut to the radial artery (inside the wrist), for example.

This leads to our second defensive principle (the first being 'awareness'). This principle is that the best on guard position is to keep your arms close to your body with the palms of your hands facing you. A cut

Incorrect guard position.

Correct guard position.

to the inside of the forearms not only risks severing the radial artery, it also risks cutting the flexor muscles, which enable you to make a fist or hold a weapon, thus making that hand severely limited in use for further defence. However, a cut to the back of the forearm avoids the major arteries and only risks cutting the extensor muscles. These muscles enable you to open your hand rather than close it, so even with a cut in this area, you may still be able to grab the opponent's arm or hold something to use as a self-defence tool.

It is unfortunate, but it has to be faced, that the reality of a knife attack may mean that you have to take a cut. If this cannot be avoided, you want your natural strategies to mean that the cut will be in the least potentially harmful place.

There is considerable advantage to be gained from quick decisive action. A person threatening you with a knife is likely to expect only fear and acquiescence from his victim, whereas a determined defensive response, as long as it is an intelligent response aimed at reducing the danger to you, is likely to cause him such shock that it would take several seconds for his thought processes to adjust to the revised situation.

Pit-al defence (beginning).

Pit-al defence (completion).

Defences and Disarming Manoeuvres

A good on guard position should also facilitate mobility and economy of movement. The two main types of initial defensive movement one can employ from the on guard position are to block or to parry. Against a powerful thrust, a block is favoured; against slashes, parries are to be preferred. Generally, slashes can change direction more easily than thrusts, and parries can track that change of trajectory more effectively than blocks.

Parrying can be done with the palm of the hand or the outer forearm. Some styles advocate the palm of the hand because it

Outside parry (beginning).

Outside parry (completion).

Edge of hand parry.

Grab and shoulder stop block.

Edge of hand block.

allows you to counter quickly with a grab, while the parry with the outer forearm is considered safer as it has a larger contact area. If you mistime the parry with the palm of the hand, the margin for error is less.

Blocking is generally done with the forearm or the hand when used as a 'shoulder stop', and is combined with grabbing the attacker's wrist and attempting to disrupt his balance. This is to allow you to establish a controlling position. Once this is achieved, the next strategy should be to strike.

Striking in a fist fight, and striking in a situation involving an edged weapon, are two entirely different situations. I have seen trained martial artists using kickboxing-type strategies in sparring exercises against training knives, and trading punches or kicks for stabs or slashes. It is easy to see who would have ended up in the worse condition. The important thing to learn in training is to do everything you can to acquire a position of 'positive control' over the opponent's knife before and while striking him. To emphasize your strike, instead of your control of his knife, is to risk the poor trade of hitting him with your hand or foot while he slashes or stabs you with his knife. The following sequence exhibits positive control of the blade whilst striking.

On-guard position.

Pit-al defence.

Elbow control.

Left cross-counter strike.

On-guard position.

Pit-al defence.

Web hand check.

Counter with elbow strike.

Once you have delivered effective strikes, a number of options should become available. Your particular situation can never be predicted, of course, for example, you may be able to wrench the arm, dislodge the knife or immobilize the attacker with a joint lock. Wrenching the elbow joint can often cause a reflexive response of the hand, which will open and can therefore result in the knife being dislodged.

It may also be possible to disarm the aggressor by the threat of pointing his own knife back towards him. The defender's controlling grip on the aggressor's wrist, and superior leverage, ensure that the aggressor cannot pass the knife to his other hand, and the blade may then be positioned to face him instead of the defender. This presents the aggressor with a huge psychological disadvantage. A common response to the fear that his own blade could be used against him is either to release the knife or to straighten the arm to push the knife away. Straightening the arm presents the defender with the options of hyper-extending the arm, dislodging the knife, or applying a joint lock.

There are four basic methods of disarming someone of a knife:

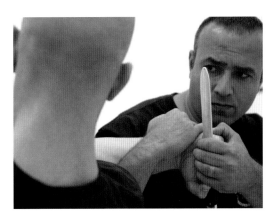

V-arm clip lock.

Figure four eagle-wing lock.

Straight arm bar lock.

Knee-supported arm bar.

Striking disarming
tactic (beginning).

Striking disarming
tactic (completed).

Forearm strip disarming
tactic (beginning).

Forearm
strip
disarming
tactic
(completed).

1. Apply a percussive strike, for example, to the knife wielder's wrist. The major advantage of this type of disarming tactic is that you do not engage the weapon directly and it should therefore reduce your chances of being cut.
2. Use the back of the forearm to strip the blade. The advantage of this disarming manoeuvre is that you do not risk cutting tendons if it goes wrong.
3. Use the webbing of the hand between the thumb and index finger. The major advantage of this disarming manoeuvre is that it allows you to retain the weapon,

Snatching disarming tactic (beginning).

Snatching disarming tactic (completed).

Pinch grip disarming tactic (beginning).

Pinch grip disarming tactic (completed).

which is a substantial advantage in deterring further conflict, for example, when faced by several potential attackers.

4. Use the 'pinch grip'. This manoeuvre is used when the blade is too short to be dislodged by the other methods.

Knife-Versus-Knife Training

The third possibility mentioned above, retaining the weapon, also touches upon why the training methods include blade versus blade and not simply unarmed defence against a knife attacker. Again it must be emphasized that this is nothing to do with encouraging the carrying of live blades or being a 'knife fighter'; rather, the emphasis is on your personal survival.

If you are unfortunate enough to be faced by more than one person, and then fortunate enough and well trained enough to take a knife away from the first attacker, it may or may not be the case that this would be sufficient to discourage the second attacker and cause him to run away. If he also draws a knife, then you, innocent victim of circumstance and *not* carrying your own knife, could very well be in a knife-versus-knife situation. You have successfully disarmed an attacker, yet you have another armed aggressor to face.

Being a law-abiding member of society would then not be enough, and only your training and experience and attributes will get you through this situation. If you have never trained for the possibility, your strategy may be inadequate to cope. It is essential to obtain proper qualified instruction, and not to hold on to the fantasy that getting no training, and carrying a knife yourself even when you know it is illegal, does anything other than increase your potential danger.

The first tactic in such a knife-versus-knife scenario is known as 'defanging the snake': this involves counter-cutting the opponent's arm as he attacks. To do this a scissoring movement called '*ginunting*' is used. The inside of the forearm is a primary target for defensive application of the knife. Remember that cutting the flexor tendons and/or associated muscles can result in an immediate loss of the ability to close the fingers, and hence grip the knife.

Remember also your legal obligation to use only 'reasonable force'. You are entitled to remove a threat, but not to take revenge upon an attacker. Thus attacking the limb can always be defended as reasonable force,

whereas stabbing the attacker in the heart may give you rather more problems (although it is not easy to anticipate what a court will regard as 'reasonable force' if you have no criminal history yourself and you were unarmed and have been attacked by two armed attackers).

It is appreciated that to target any part of the body precisely in highly stressful circumstances is easier to talk about than to control. A cut higher up the attacker's arm may sever his biceps and severely hinder coordinated motion of that arm.

A cut on the outside of his arm may sever the triceps muscle or the triceps tendon above the elbow, again affecting or removing the ability to extend and coordinate movement of the arm and his ability to wield his own weapon effectively.

If he tries to kick you, you may respond with a cut to the quadriceps. This may very well remove his support and mobility, without having severed the femoral artery (again quickly fatal), which may enable you to make an escape without him being able to give pursuit. (You would be unlikely to hit the femoral artery without deliberately, and homicidally, targeting it, and it is assumed here that your intentions are, and should be, wholly defensive.)

On-guard position.

Bicep *ginunting*.

Training Drills

In order to effectively apply techniques at realistic speeds, the eskrimador needs to have well honed attributes. In terms of knife defence, the main attribute to develop is tactile sensitivity. At close quarters, the knife may move too fast to be tracked by the eyes, and therefore the hands and forearms have to be able to 'feel' the opponent's intentions. This attribute is developed through knife-tapping flow drills, commonly called *pit-al* or *tapi-tapi*.

Pit-al (meaning to press) is a drill whereby the defender uses the outer part of the forearm to defend against knife attacks. The idea is to maintain contact with a forward pressing movement, similar to a corkscrew action. The *pit-al* movement is ideal for dealing with those attacks that change level (for example, high to low). However, there are occasions when constant forearm contact cannot be maintained by the defender. One example is when the attacker clears the defender's arm with a tapping motion: this is called *tapi-tapi* (loosely translated as 'knife tapping'). The following drill teaches the defender to momentarily and automatically react with his free hand when the attacker clears the defender's initial *pit-al* movement. The role of the free hand is to block temporarily the opponent's attack, 'buying time' for the other hand to disengage and re-establish the *pit-al* position.

Pit-al tapi.

Web hand check.

Half-beat palm strike.

Pit-al tapi.

Web hand check.

Pit-al tapi.

Web hand check.

Pit-al tapi.

Web hand check.

Knife Sparring

Knife-versus-knife sparring is an excellent training method for developing footwork, speed, timing and quick reflexes. Always use safe training knives and wear eye protection. After knife sparring, sparring with empty hands will feel 'slower' in comparison, since the knife is quicker than the hand or foot, and you will have a lot more reaction time.

Conclusion

If after a real encounter you get what you think is a superficial cut yourself, never assume that the knife was clean and that there is no danger to your health. Get medical attention, as the cut could be infected. If you do not, in as little as twenty-four hours your cut limb could be seriously in danger of amputation.

If you encounter the victim of a knife attack, then apart from ensuring that they are breathing and not bleeding to death, it is vital to obtain professional medical attention as quickly as possible. A knife, if still sticking in the body, must not be removed from a wound: you could do as much damage on

Knife sparring (looking for opening).

Use safe padded knives when sparring.

Knife sparring (hand cut).

the way out as the attacker did on the way in. It is strongly recommended that, if you are not a medical professional, you take a first aid course as well as martial arts lessons.

These all seem to be very serious matters. It should perhaps finally be emphasized that just as the enjoyment of fencing is not about 'killing people with swords', the appreciation of knife training is not about the tragedy of innocent victims of dreadful crimes, or about being paranoid and exaggerating the risk of being the victim of a knife threat. The training methods involve sensitivity, enhanced coordination, awareness, reflex improvement, technical understanding and speed, and the richness and intelligence of Filipino knife defence training brings enormous pleasure and benefits to its practitioners. When it saves a few innocent lives along the way, that is a bonus.

As a martial art, Eskrima advocates the notion that fighting only leads to war and death, not peace. Its world view is that man

in his relationship with man will always find himself in contentious situations. The paradigm of this relationship is one of entering into a dialogue or discourse with three objectives in mind:

1. Avoid conflict at all times.
2. Aim at achieving cooperation.
3. Try to settle for a compromise.

However, the system as a fighting art also recognizes that conflict is sometimes inevitable. In extreme circumstances, in order to preserve your life or the life of a loved one, you have to face the reality of violence and danger. You may even be faced with the drastic possibility of having taken the life of another. No one else can have your experiences, or your conscience. No martial art has a magic wand to protect you from harm – or from bad luck, or from guilt, or from legal interpretations in a courtroom after the event. It can only help you to increase the statistical chances in favour of your survival. It is better to be around to take part in any dispute about what happened and who did, or should have done what, than it is to be an innocent but dead victim, with a grieving family and friends.

5 *Pangamut* – Empty Hands

This chapter will focus on hand-to-hand combat, as opposed to empty hands versus weapons, as this is covered in the other relevant chapters.

In many martial arts, the students are taught unarmed or empty-hand techniques first. Later, they are taught to use the weapon as an extension of the limb, so that the weapon principles are derived from the empty-hand movement principles. The Filipino martial arts take the opposite approach, as they are weapons-based systems. There are historical and cultural reasons for this. If you live in a place where a physical encounter is likely to lead to someone drawing a knife on you, then it makes little sense to spend several years learning how to defend against purely unarmed attacks,

only to find yourself poorly prepared for dealing with a weapon. It is therefore regarded as logical to teach the use of, and defence against, weapons from the earliest stages of training. The movement principles of the empty-hand techniques are then derived or translated from the movements used with weaponry, instead of the other way round.

Depending on which style or system you are studying, the weaponry from which the empty hands have been derived will vary. Some styles will derive/translate their movements from that of the knife, whilst others will get it from the double stick. The following photographs show empty-hand movement translated from a double-stick pattern called *sinawali*.

Ready posture.

Inside parry versus jab.

Outside parry versus cross.

Counter with backhand chop.

Pangamut – also spelt *pangamot* – means 'bare hands' or 'empty hands'. Within the broader term *pangamut* you have the following three sub-systems:

1. *Panantukan/Suntukan.*
2. *Pananjakman/Sikaran/Sipa.*
3. *Dumog.*

This chapter focuses predominately on *panantukan*, but an introduction to *pananjakman* and *dumog* is also given. *Panantukan* is also called *suntukan* in the Tagalog dialect. *Panantukan* is an old Visayan word meaning 'punching' or 'striking'; in the West it is more popularly known as 'Filipino boxing'. As this term suggests, it has a lot of similarities to Western boxing, and therefore in order to understand the origins of *panantukan* we need to look first at the origins of Western boxing.

The Evolution of Western Boxing

The largest obstacle facing Filipino martial artists is the lack of written documentation regarding the technical evolution of their art. The earliest surviving instructional manual

on the art is Placido Yambao's *Mga Karunungan sa Laring Arnis* (1957). However, this is a book focusing on classical *espada y daga* as opposed to empty hands. A copy of Don Baltazar Gonzales' book *De los Delitos* (1800) remains to be found, according to the late Grandmaster Eulogio 'Yoling' Cañete – this book made references to *pangamut* (empty hands). According to Grandmaster Abner Pasa, the only copy that Yoling saw was destroyed during World War II. As a result we must rely on oral tradition, which some critics regard as unreliable.

In contrast, about twenty instructional Western boxing manuals were published before 1850. Since 1850, over 200 instructional manuals are known. This allows us to trace the early evolution of the art through literature. Some years ago, I spent a considerable amount of time analysing most of these manuals in the British Museum library; these are my thoughts on the evolution of Western boxing.

Early boxing in England (1740–80) was somewhat crude and highly individual. Footwork was meagre – the only individual to have used it to any great extent during this period was Ned Hunt, a pupil of Broughton (the father of modern boxing). Broughton was extremely proficient at body punching, and the solar plexus was often referred to as Broughton's 'mark'. During this period, chops with the hammer fist and swings were widely used. Defence was essentially guarding with the forearm. The forearms were used to deflect straight punches, and to block swings and chops. Counter attacks called 'returns' were made *after* the initial attack was complete. Straight punches that used a modified fencing lunge so as to throw the body's weight into the punch were known from the earliest period. The stance was the same as that of English single-stick play, in which many boxers of this period cross-trained.

In the 1780s, the great pugilist Daniel Mendoza did much to evolve boxing footwork, and retreating and side-stepping gradually began to lose their overtones of cowardice. 'Gentleman' John Jackson perfected the straight left lead in 1790, and used it with authority. During the same period Ben Brain fathered the straight right, and Dutch Sam introduced the uppercut in 1800. The hook punch was hardly used: because it is a short-range blow, the hook would more easily expose its user to a close and throw.

Throws played a great part in the fights of this era; cross-buttocks (high hip throws) and a variety of trips such as the back heel were common. Fighters often 'accidentally' fell on their opponent so as to maximize the impact of the throw. 'Fibbing' – later called 'head in chancery' – (holding the opponent's head with one hand while hitting it with the other) was widely practised. Defensive hitting (the ability to hit effectively whilst retreating) was known during this period, but was called 'milling on the retreat'. It was developed by Tom Cribb in 1810.

At some time during the 1840s the on guard position changed. Perhaps the decrease in boxers cross-training with weaponry (principally single stick) influenced this development. The hands were lowered (note: not always to their detriment), the left pointing forward and the right held across the mark (solar plexus). The stance was more upright, sometimes effaced and sometimes with the shoulders square. The lower guard led to the development of 'head movement' – slipping, ducking and swaying back. It also contributed to the development of 'drawing'. 'Counters' (counter-attacks delivered simultaneously with the attack) were also developed during the mid-1800s.

It is interesting to note that under Broughton's rules (1743), and the rules of the London Prize Ring (1838, 1853), few blows were barred, wrestling was allowed, and the fight continued until one man or the other could no longer rise ('toe the scratch') or be dragged to his feet at the end of thirty seconds. The Marquis of Queensberry rules (1867) introduced the wearing of gloves for fights (although they were known as 'mufflers' and were worn for sparring since Broughton's time). The Queensberry rules also introduced the 3-minute round and the 10-second knockout. This further changed the shape of boxing, and in some cases it increased the severity of professional fights, for gloves protect a fighter's hands more than his opponent's face.

Swings became popular again, because the protection provided by the gloves helped reduce the risk of damage to the hands when delivering these punches. James J. Corbett was credited with developing the short or 'shovel' hook in 1889. In the same year George La Blanche knocked out the original Jack Dempsey with the 'pivot punch' (in martial arts parlance 'spinning backfist'), a move taught to him by the English lightweight Jimmy Carroll. The 'corkscrew blow', which involved rotation of the fist from palm up to palm down, was popularized during the 1890s by Kid McCoy (although it was originally taught to him by the great trainer Jimmy DeForest). The Queensberry rules banned wrestling, and as a result the natural crouch gained in popularity, and was used effectively by such fighters as Frank Slavin and Jim Jeffries.

During the early 1900s, Jack Johnson, the greatest defensive boxer of that time period, perfected the 'catch', a defensive manoeuvre whereby you literally catch the opponent's punch in the palm of your glove. 'In-fighting' was also developed considerably during the early 1900s. The 'bob and weave' – also known as 'rolling' – was used more often to get into close quarters and gain the 'inside position'. Concepts such as 'shifting' with the opponent's punches, and different types of clinching, were developed.

Panantukan

Western boxing came to the Philippines (via US servicemen) in the late nineteenth and early twentieth centuries. As can be seen from the above, it was already a highly evolved art. Guro Dan Inosanto has mentioned that 'when the Americans saw the Filipinos box (early 1900s) they noticed a high on-guard position, unusually quick punching and lots of footwork; unknown to them this was as a result of previous training with the knife.'

In my archives I have a boxing article called 'The Father of Philippine Boxing' (1927); the article is about Eddie Tait, one of the first boxing promoters in the Philippines. It contains some interesting observations, such as '…there has been a gradual discarding of the deadly knife, without which the average Filipino once thought himself hardly dressed'. It should be noted that not many discarded the knife – even today, many of the Philippine islands retain a blade culture, and I believe it is the influence of the knife which makes *panantukan* unique.

I trained extensively with Manong Estaneslao 'Tanny' del Campo. Tanny was one of the best boxers to come out of the Philippines. He fought for the world bantamweight title in the 1950s, and fought two very close fights against the legendary Gabriel 'Flash' Elorde, largely regarded as the best Filipino boxer in history. Tanny told me the Filipino method of boxing differs from Western boxing in the following ways:

> It is essentially a bare-fist art. It makes use of punches to the groin, elbows to the body and face, arm wrenching, head butting, and 'turning' or 'spinning' the opponent so as to disorientate him. The parry is favoured against the block, because your opponent may be attacking with a concealed weapon in the fist. In short it is designed for the street. If you want to box in the ring, you must learn Western boxing, because if you use *Pangamut* in the ring you will surely get disqualified.

Pangamut legend – *Estaneslao 'Tanny' del Campo.*

Reverse grip slash.

Elbow strike.

Reverse grip stab.

Hammer-fist strike.

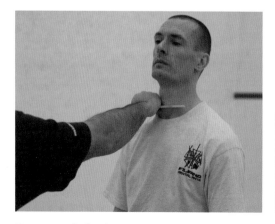

Reverse grip hack.

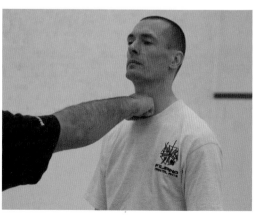

Throat punch.

It seems that the Filipinos must have embraced Western boxing, and then applied their knowledge of the knife to create a similar yet distinct art. The following are some examples of the relationship between knife motions and empty-hand translations. When the knife is held in the reverse grip, any slashing motion can be translated into an elbow strike, while any thrusting motion can be translated into a hammer-fist strike. Also, when gripped in the reverse grip, if the knife is used to hack, then this translates directly to empty-hand punching techniques.

Although the modern cross-cultural influences mean that there is considerable overlap with the kind of boxing techniques and training methods taught in, for example, Western or Thai boxing, *panantukan* was never designed as a sport, but for street self-defence. It includes open-hand strikes and close-range methods such as elbows, and it blends into other aspects of combat such as bone breaking, locking and unbalancing. It is therefore important to appreciate that different types of training are necessary, both with and without the use of boxing gloves, in order to acquire the full range of skills.

Training with Boxing Gloves and Focus Mitts

To acquire any striking power, and to cope with the resulting effects on the joints and the balance and momentum of the body, it is necessary to strike targets. Focus mitts (and indeed heavy bags) are ideal for combining this need to acquire striking power with flexibility of method and movement.

The beginner is likely to be introduced to this training by using the hands and fists only, first, in single strikes and then in combinations. A method frequently encountered in FMA training is to use a three-count combination, which can be trained in many ways and with different rhythms and footwork, providing a more realistic 'feel' for the technique than stop-start attack-and-defence combinations.

Body movement is probably the next most important aspect of the training, starting with basic footwork and distance judgement, enabling closing with an attacker or evading an attack. It is vital for the student to combine body mobility with striking power. This then leads into the more subtle mobility principles of ducking, swaying back, slipping a punch, and using the bob and weave.

These all have to be trained separately and intelligently, and with full awareness of the dangers of, for example, losing your own balance through over-commitment, or using an evasive movement that would be fine under Western boxing rules but not in the street, where your attacker can use his knees. The basic skills of punching and footwork and body movement can then be enhanced by the addition of kicks, and then knees and elbows, to the training drills.

In order to ensure again that the training remains safe, progressive and intelligent, the student will then need to learn to cope with a coach who is no longer only providing targets to hit, while the student himself is concentrating on his own striking power and movement and needs to be not under threat. The good coach then becomes a dynamic part of the whole process.

The coach can next introduce 'reaction and recovery' training, where the student is presented with unpredictable angles to attack, and has to react appropriately and quickly and then recover his guard position. He is sometimes presented with a pad which is moved before he can hit it, the coach deliberately wanting him to miss rather than hit. Now, instead of only training striking power, he is correcting any tendency to over-commit, which will sacrifice recovery, defence and flexibility of response, and leave the student open to counters.

Some methods of using focus mitts to improve striking speed may be unique to the Filipino martial arts, such as concentrating on the retraction-only half of the punch, and the coach holding a training dagger in his other hand to try and simulate a cut to the punching arm immediately after it has hit the pad.

For example, let's take the jab. Hold a focus pad in your right hand, and a knife in your left hand. If the puncher drops the arm upon retraction, hold the knife at chest level. This will give him feedback. If the punching arm is slow to retract after hitting the pad, cut it with the knife. If the puncher has a tendency to lean 'over' the central axis when punching with the right cross, put the knife in front of the sternum – this will make him rotate his torso 'around' the central axis. If you want to increase speed of footwork, get the puncher to move into range with the jab

and stab the lead leg, so that he moves rapidly out of range – after jabbing.

The coach will then become a responsive training partner, moving around, occasionally using a focus mitt (or his own gloves) to simulate an attack rather than a target. This ensures that the student will always be ready to cover up, to guard, to bob and weave or to otherwise avoid.

This type of training then leads in to sparring. Sparring training is often misunderstood, and treated as if it were the same as a competition. In a competition, however, you are simply trying to win, and to hurt your opponent. In sparring training, you are supposed to train *with* rather than on

Coaching technique to ensure the punching arm does not drop upon retraction.

Close-up of the above.

Coaching technique to develop explosive footwork for moving out of the opponent's striking distance.

Coaching technique to develop speed in retraction of a punch.

your partner. It is a process of mutual improvement and skill development, where you can train to use different themes or strategies, rather than just 'scoring a point' or 'winning'.

The idea should be to drill smoothly rather than hard, starting off by alternating in a counter-for-counter approach, ensuring that you are both working on your guard and your reflexes while working for spontaneity and variety. There can be a series of themed rounds, for example where both people can use only one hand, or can use both hands, but no footwork; you could deliberately choose to be using high-low attacks and low-high attacks; you could have a round concentrating on using, avoiding and countering elbow strikes. You could try different methods of using combinations – for example, you start every combination with a fake, or you finish every combination with a jab and a retreat.

This gives you the opportunity to isolate different skills and strategies. Concentrating on using fakes, for example, will reveal whether your apparent commitment is convincing enough to produce the desired defensive response. If you are constantly falling for a strategy of your opponent, or you are making *him* fall for something you do, then this is a good illustration of why this is almost the opposite of a competition. In a competition you *want* to fool him and be the successful one, whereas in sparring training you should *want* to show your opponent how to improve, one principle at a time. You then have to take another step up the technical ladder in finding a different way of getting your attacks to work. This can only improve the skills and understanding of everyone involved.

For self-defence training, it is also important to train sparring situations with more than one attacker; this will help develop quick, mobile and evasive footwork. Zoning and using one attacker as a shield against the others becomes critical. The jab becomes the essential punch as it can be thrown whilst 'on the move'.

Training Without Boxing Gloves

Remembering that *panantukan* is not Western boxing, it is at least as important to engage in training methods that do not involve the use of gloves or impact. This is partly because there are practical fighting tactics that are either hampered or prevented by gloves, and/or methods that may be outside Western boxing. It is also to enhance the development of forearm sensitivity, and the fine awareness of open lines that are even more important when facing a knife than when facing an unarmed opponent (as a knife can get into a smaller gap than a fist).

'Split entry' knife thrust.

'Split entry' finger jab.

Examples of such tactics and training methods would include the 'split entry' (where one hand is outside and one inside the attacking limb of the opponent), as demonstrated in the photographs.

It would also include using the open hand in a scooping movement to offset an opponent and to create an opening or to prevent a counter-attack, while setting up a follow-up that may be an elbow strike, a wrench, or a lock: see the accompanying photographs.

It could also mean offsetting the opponent's balance by moving his upper body while 'foot sectoring' – that is, positioning one of your feet inside or outside one of his,

Reverse grip 'scoop' (beginning).

Reverse grip 'scoop' (completion).

Elbow destruction to the bicep.

Scoop (beginning).

Scoop (completion).

with the object of preventing him moving a foot to recover his balance, or to assist you with a sweep or trip.

To train arm sensitivity, a training drill known as '*higut hubad*', or usually just '*hubad*', is used, *hubad* meaning to untie, and *higut* to tie. The name is descriptive of one person's attempt to trap or 'tie up' the opponent's arms, whilst the other 'unties' himself. (If intending to train in the Philippines, take care to avoid offence with this, as *hubad* means 'untie' in the Visayan dialect, but 'undress' in another dialect.)

This drill has as its foundation a basic four-count shell (block or parry – raise – trap – hit), and therefore its essence is very simple to learn. It is, however, extremely useful and flexible, as various other methods and tactics can be 'attached' to this shell. These

Very rare photo of GM Venancio 'Ansiong' Bacon applying foot sectoring technique.

Foot sector number 1.

Foot sector number 2.

Foot sector number 3.

Foot sector number 4.

On-guard position.

Reverse grip – fist slash.

Reverse grip – fist stab.

include methods of changing sides (to train both left and right), usually using a circling or disconnecting movement, and it can then be used to practise trapping, locking, choking, unbalancing and 'limb destruction' techniques.

Because of its fundamental repetitive structure this drill therefore not only becomes a safe method of developing flow from one movement to another, but also provides the opportunity for dozens of repetitions of fundamental technique, creating the automatic 'muscle memory' and nervous-system reflexes required in a self-defence situation.

The concept of awareness of open lines of attack, and of using fakes or deceptive movements to create open lines, is related to the concept of 'trapping'. It may be important either to remove an obstruction (something in the way of your desired target), or simply to restrict an opponent's possible counters: closing off at least one of *his* lines may be what provides the possibility of *your* attack succeeding. A trap is often a simple idea, based on a push (or slap), or a pull, or perhaps the use of a guarding hand while circling your hand around an obstructing limb and/or moving your head or body to a safer position. However, the required tactics and sensitivity can only be trained through such appropriate unarmed training drills.

The concept of what is known as 'limb destruction' originates in the thinking and attitudes of a knife-fighter rather than a boxer. If you are 'only' a boxer, then you have to get past the opponent's weapons and his guard (his limbs) in order to reach your targets (his head and body). With a knife in your hand, however, anything that an attacker puts within your reach becomes *your target* instead of *his* weapon – because it does not matter to you that it is a hand or arm, because if you can reach it, you can cut it or stab it. The following example shows the use of the limb destruction concept in a reverse grip:

Elbow destruction to fist.

Elbow 'spike' to fist.

When you are unarmed, as in the normal self-defence situation, then this psychology and strategy can still be applied: instead of having a knife, you have your knuckles and elbows and fingers. However, you can still take the psychological approach that if you can reach it, you can hurt it. If your oppnent's limbs are offered, and/or if more serious targets are out of reach, they are legitimate targets for your elbows and hands. As an example, an elbow strike to the knuckles of a punching hand, or to the muscles of the arm, can be devastatingly painful to the puncher. It therefore 'destroys the limb' – that is, takes it out of action temporarily – and makes it possible for you to attack another target (if that is not sufficiently discouraging to the attacker) to remove the threat. The photographs show how to use the elbows in a seemingly 'defensive' manner to destroy a straight punching attack.

This also has the advantage that, even if the opponent has the apparent advantage of a longer reach, as long as you have enough awareness of distance, he cannot reach his intended target (which is likely to be your body or head), while you can reach (and strike) anything within range (starting with his nearest limb).

Another form of limb attack is the arm wrench, opportunities for which may appear more frequently than is often realized in practical situations. One of your hands or arms is likely to be providing resistance (or a fulcrum) in the region of the opponent's wrist, while the other hand (or arm, or part of your body) would be providing pressure against his elbow, in the opposite direction from the normal angle in which it bends. Whether this pressure is towards you, away from you, or upwards or downwards, depends entirely on your relative positions and the nature of the situation.

Although called 'limb destructions', such techniques are likely to be relatively minor attacks, perhaps as part of the opening moves of an encounter, rather than being as 'destructive' as the name implies. They are also an extremely moral way of attempting to deal with an attack, in that they do not cause bleeding, they do not attack the brain or any major organs, and they may prevent further attack and discourage an attacker without having caused him any serious or permanent damage. This may be extremely important in a complicated situation, where perhaps you need to defend yourself against any false counter-accusation that you had initiated the conflict, or any claim that you were using 'unreasonable force'.

Knife *ginunting* to bicep.

Knuckle *ginunting* to bicep.

There is a variety of ways of training limb destruction techniques. They should arise 'naturally', from whatever your hand positions are, relative to his punching arm. Your hands may be down, or one of them may be inside or outside the attacking limb, for example, and there is likely to be no time to move your hand to a different sector before using it to strike with.

The following examples show how to attack the bicep with a knife – a thrust motion is used – while with the empty hands, the knuckles are used to attack the muscle or the ulna nerve.

An attack to the limb may therefore be used:

• against an initial attack;
• to intercept a combination, for example if you have avoided the first attack with a reflexive head movement but without time for an immediate counter-strike;
• or to cause relatively minor pain or distraction in order to set up, or give you the opportunity for, a major strike to a more 'serious' target where this is still required.

Pananjakman

Sikaran/sipa/pananjakman are some of the names used by various systems/styles to describe the Filipino method of kicking. The word *sipa* actually means 'kick' in Tagalog, and *pananjakman* is an old Visayan word meaning 'kicking'.

From a combative perspective, the kicks are all delivered on the low line – that is, anywhere below the groin. Low kicks allow you to retain better balance, to minimize the opponent's ability to grab your leg and, when used in conjunction with weaponry, safeguard your leg from being hit with the *punyo* or stabbed with a knife. We do use 'head' kicks, but not in the conventional sense: head kicks are used when the opponent's head is clinched and lowered to a safe level. The following photographs show the use of low kicks in different ranges.

Dumog

Dumog is the Filipino term for wrestling/grappling. It encompasses various manoeuvres including takedowns, joint locks, chokes and strangles. Takedowns are effected by breaking the opponent's balance; this involves both pulling the arms and pushing the shoulders, manipulating the opponent's head, and sweeping the legs.

Joint locks are applied to the fingers, wrist, elbow and shoulder. Often these locks are

Rare photo of GM Frederico 'Digoy' Veraye demonstrating side kick to knee.

Upward heel kick to groin.

Upward heel kick to face.

Heel hook kick to knee.

Upward front kick to groin.

Oblique kick to knee.

taught in the form of a 'lock flow' (*luyog*) – a series of locks that flow smoothly from one to the other, the idea being that as the opponent gets out of one lock attempt, you can flow into another.

The following sequence is a simple five-count lock flow, which teaches how to flow from a wrist lock, to elbow locks, to shoulder locks.

Chokes and strangles are attacks to the neck, and are normally used to restrain a person. Chokes work on stopping the air flow, usually by means of pressure from the forearm against the front of the throat (although the situation may mean that this

Wrist lock.

V arm clip lock.

Reverse V arm clip lock.

Figure four straight arm lock.

Breast pin lock.

pressure is being applied by a hand or, say, a shin), while strangles restrict the flow of blood to the brain, by pressure on the arteries at the side of the neck.

When training chokes and strangles, it is vitally important to use the 'tapping' submission, and for all participants to respect this and immediately release the pressure. It is extremely foolish to try and 'tough it out' in an attempt to increase the amount of time that such an attack could be 'tolerated' by the body. This does not lead to a 'tougher fighter', but to unconsciousness and the possibility of serious organic damage. Even when both training partners are aware of tapping, however, care is still needed because you do not necessarily know that you are about to pass out, so it is reasonably easy to go unconscious without having tapped first.

In a self-defence situation, however, such techniques can be extremely useful, and again can demonstrate the intention of a fundamentally moral approach that does not use 'unreasonable force'. It may be necessary, for example, to be holding one person in a manner that seriously restricts his ability to hurt you, while using him as a shield between you and a second attacker. The nature of the situation may have led you into a choke position rather than an arm-lock position. It is also far safer to strangle an attacker into unconsciousness, but not to death of course, than it is to cause potential damage to the brain with impact strikes to the head.

Please note that chokes are more dangerous than strangles because it is possible to damage the windpipe, and as a result the person may not be able to breathe even after you have taken the pressure away. A strangle is far more likely simply to mean unconsciousness and then full recovery, with virtually no risk of permanent damage (as long as the pressure is not unduly maintained). However, this does not mean that chokes are too dangerous to train: they

Rare photo of GM Frederico 'Digoy' Veraye demonstrating the choke hold.

have been trained perfectly safely many hundreds of thousands of times in, for example, judo and jujitsu, for centuries. Nevertheless the instructor must always have sufficiently responsible awareness of the potential dangers.

In the following three techniques, note how one of the opponent's arms is controlled whilst the strangle or choke is applied. This is critical when faced with an edged weapon – you must maintain positive control of the blade whilst applying the technique. Therefore, a choke or strangle that commits both hands to the manoeuvre works well in an unarmed conflict, but is not appropriate when defending against an edged weapon.

It remains advisable, in a self-defence situation, to maintain 'weapons awareness'. Even if you have not yet seen a weapon or a second attacker, you should assume that there may very well be at least one. If you become obsessed with trying to grapple with one person at close range in order to acquire a choke or arm-lock restraint position, you could become more vulnerable to a potentially fatal blow, either from a weapon drawn by him during the tussling, or by another person you have not 'yet' seen.

If you have choked or strangled someone into unconsciousness, and if they remain unconscious for longer than a mere 15 seconds or so, then as long as the situation makes it possible for you to do this without being in further danger yourself, it may become necessary to take measures to preserve the person's life. They must not be left on their back (unless you have established that they are not breathing and you are applying CPR).

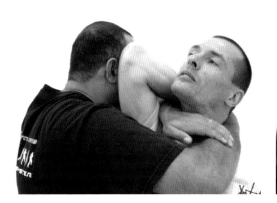

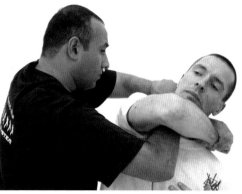

ABOVE: Side strangle.

TOP LEFT: Front strangle.

LEFT: Rear choke and arm bar.

6 *Doble Baston* – Double Stick

Once some basic familiarity has been acquired with the stick and the knife separately, skills can be enhanced further by training with multiple weapons. This is really more than one area of training, because of the different characteristics and strategies appropriate to different weapons. 'Multiple weapons' could mean the use of double sticks, or of a stick in one hand and a knife in the other, or of double daggers, or of a sword and shield.

Broadly speaking, double-stick training can be categorized into three areas: coordination drills, flow drills and combat techniques. Each area develops different skills and attributes; I teach the double stick progression in the above order as I feel it better facilitates ease of learning for the student, but some styles may not teach all three areas, and some focus on one particular category as an area of specialization.

Coordination Drills

Coordination drills are practised to improve your non-dominant side: for 87 per cent of the population that is the left. These drills are generally characterized by both individuals doing the same movement at the same time. The practitioners 'hit sticks' to develop a sense of rhythm and timing. However, it should be noted that the movements being practised do retain a practical application; it's just that when practised in the context of hitting sticks, the main goal is to develop better coordination and synchronization between the two arms.

The basic single stick coordination drills are known as *kob kob* and *sinawali*. *Kob Kob* is trained from an 'open chamber', with one stick held on each side of the body. *Sinawali* means 'weaving', and starts from a 'closed chamber', with both sticks on the same side of the body, one over the arm and one under the arm. It is also possible to train drills using a 'parallel position', where the sticks are again on the same side of the body, but this time they are both over or both under the arm.

Sinawali is common to all Filipino martial arts styles that use double stick. It has many variations, but basically uses cross-over attacks, going under and over each arm, from a fundamental six-count structure. It can then use a mixture of high and low angles of attack, and variations using thrusts or reverse grips with either or both of the sticks. Slightly different variations of coordination are developed with five-count drills.

Open chamber.

Closed chamber.

Parallel chamber.

Chambers

Coordination drills are usually practised from three chambers, these being *abierta* (open), *serrada* (closed) and the parallel chamber.

Kob Kob/Pingke Pingke

The easiest progression is to start with the open chamber; a good drill to work from this chamber is called *kob kob*, or *pingke pingke*. This drill consists of the downward X (*equis*) strike, the upward figure-eight strike (*ocho-ocho*), the high-low-high strike, and the jab strike. As with any movement, make sure that you are bringing your hips into play when striking, as this ensures correct body mechanics.

The following sequence exhibits this drill:

On-guard – open chamber.

Forehand slash (right arm).

Backhand slash (right arm).

Re-chamber.

Forehand slash (left arm).

Follow-through.

Backhand slash (left arm).

Re-chamber.

Palm up uppercut (right arm).

Follow-through.

Palm down uppercut (right arm).

Re-chamber.

Palm up uppercut (left arm).

Follow through.

Palm down uppercut (left arm).

Re-chamber.

Forehand slash high (right arm).

Follow-through.

Low backhand jab (right arm).

Retract strike.

High backhand slash (right arm).

Re-chamber.

Forehand slash high (left arm).

Follow-through.

Low backhand jab (left arm).

Retract strike.

High backhand slash (left arm).

Re-chamber.

High forehand jab (right arm).

Retract strike.

High forehand jab (left arm).

Mid-uppercut jab (right arm).

Retract strike.

Mid-uppercut jab (left arm).

Retract strike.

Low forehand jab (right arm).

Retract strike.

Low forehand jab (left arm).

Retract strike (end of drill).

Sinawali

The next drill to work is from the closed chamber, and is called *sinawali*. *Sinawali* means 'to weave', and is descriptive of how the arms weave in and out when practising this movement. When practised as a coordination drill, the first two movements are slashes (strikes that follow through), and the third is a retracting jab strike.

There are eight basic variations to this drill, which can be abbreviated as follows:

H = High, or head
L = Low, or leg

1. HHH
2. HHL
3. HLL
4. HLH
5. LLL
6. LLH
7. LHH
8. LHL.

The standard way to practise this drill is to strike with the *top* stick first, although at a

later stage when your coordination is better, you can also begin the sequence with the *bottom* stick. Therefore, you begin by 'matching' your opponent's strike, then at a later stage you can 'mirror' it.

The following sequence exhibits this drill; note that due to space limitations only half of the pattern is shown. When you are practising, just remember to replicate the movements the other way round, starting on the opposite side of the body.

Closed chamber.

High forehand slash (right arm).

Follow-through.

High backhand slash (left arm).

Follow-through.

High jab strike (right arm).

Re-chamber on the left side, and repeat the sequence the other way round.

Closed chamber.

High forehand slash (right arm).

Follow-through.

Low backhand slash (left arm).

Follow-through.

High jab strike (right arm).

Re-chamber on the left side, and repeat the sequence the other way round.

Closed chamber.

Low forehand slash (right arm).

Follow-through.

Low backhand slash (left arm).

Follow-through.

Low jab strike (right arm).

Re-chamber on the left side and repeat the sequence the other way round.

Closed chamber.

Low forehand slash (right arm).

Follow-through.

High backhand slash (left arm).

Follow-through.

Low jab strike (right arm).

Re-chamber on the left side and repeat the sequence the other way round.

Closed chamber.

Once the basic 'alternating' three-count drills have been installed, you can progress to a five-count. The following example is called five-count 'switch', because it teaches you to switch hand positions. For illustrative purposes only half of the drill is shown, so remember to practise it in exactly the same way, but the other way round.

High forehand jab (left arm).

Low backhand jab (right arm).

Low forehand jab (left arm); simultaneously chamber your right arm on your left shoulder.

High backhand slash (right arm).

High forehand slash (left arm).

Re-chamber on the right side and repeat the sequence the other way round.

Flow Drills – Counter for Counter

Once you are comfortable with the coordination drills, the next stage is to practise flow drills. These differ from the coordination drills in that they are counter for counter, whilst in the coordination drills you mirror your partner's strikes. These flow drills start to develop your reactions, because after striking you have to quickly recover with a defence. Also, they require higher levels of coordination and consequently are taught to the student once the basic *Sinawali drills* are performed fluently.

Sombrada

There are numerous drills in this category, such as *sombrada* (also spelt *sumbrada*), *pakgang*, and so on. To illustrate all of them is beyond the scope of this book, but the following example is called *doble baston – sombrada*, *sombrada* meaning 'to shadow'. It is a descriptive term for 'shadowing' your partner in a counter-for-counter fashion.

The following sequence exhibits this drill:

On-guard position.

Defend the forehead strike with the roof block.

Chamber the right stick to feed the forehand slash.

Block the forehand slash to the temple.

Ritirada step to avoid a leg strike with a simultaneous drop-stick block.

Block a thrust to the abdomen, and simultaneously chamber the stick on the left shoulder.

Block the backhand slash with the reverse roof block.

Defend the forehead strike with the roof block.

Block the forehand slash to the temple.

A *ritirada* step to avoid a leg strike with simultaneous drop-stick block.

Block a thrust to the abdomen, and simultaneously chamber the stick on the left shoulder.

Block the backhand slash with the reverse roof block.

Combat Techniques

These are techniques that you would use in sparring. One of the most efficient and effective tactics in double stick sparring is to use one stick for defence and simultaneously attack with the other stick. This can be done either by you initiating the strike, or your opponent leads and you counter attack.

Ginunting

One of the 'styles' that teaches this type of technique is the *ginunting* (often abbreviated as *gunting*) method. *Ginunting* means 'scissor', and is descriptive of the opening and closing movement of a scissor that resembles this technique. It is a counter-attacking method, whereby a 'false' opening is presented in order to 'draw' the opponent's attack. This is either parried or blocked, while the free stick simultaneously strikes the opponent's arm, the goal being to efficiently disarm your opponent's weapons.

The following sequence exhibits this drill:

Draw the opponent's angle no. 1 strike with the *ginunting* chamber.

Simultaneously counter with the left parry and right-hand smash.

Use the crossed *ginunting* chamber to draw the opponent's angle no. 2 strike.

Block the leg strike and simultaneously counter with the left-hand smash.

Draw the opponent's angle no. 3 strike with the *ginunting* chamber.

Simultaneously counter with a left parry and right-hand smash.

Use a crossed *ginunting* chamber to draw the opponent's angle no. 4 strike.

Block the head strike and simultaneously counter with the left-hand smash.

Draw the opponent's angle no. 5 strike with the *ginunting* chamber.

Simultaneously counter with a left parry and right-hand smash.

Note that the *ginunting* is an 'entry' technique, and you should practise 'following up' with a combination of strikes. The follow up can consist of striking patterns learnt previously such as *pingke pingke* (*kob kob*) or *sinawali*.

Combat *Sonkite*

Sonkite, also spelt *sunkit*, means 'thrust'. The following sequence shows how you can close in on an opponent, and create openings for thrusting techniques. Note how the opponent's attempts at blocking eventually lead to her sticks being trapped.

Draw the opponent's strike with the *ginunting* chamber.

Defend with the reverse roof block.

Counter with a backhand slash, the opponent blocks.

Counter with a centre line thrust to the eye.

The opponent parries your thrust, you simultaneously chamber the right stick for a forehand slash.

Counter with a forehand slash to the jaw.

Trap the opponent's sticks and simultaneously chamber for a thrust.

Finish with a thrust to the opponent's throat.

Combat *Pluma y Payong*

Pluma means 'pen' and *payong* means 'umbrella'. *Pluma* is the reverse of *payong* in that the palm of your hand is facing up, whilst the palm is facing down with the *payong* motion. In the following sequence, the *pluma* is used as a shielding movement and the *payong* as a block. If the *payong* block is circled around the head, it offers full protection similar to an umbrella.

Draw the opponent's backhand slash.

Simultaneously counter with a block and upward eye thrust.

Use *pluma* to disengage the right stick.

Counter with a hand smash.

Use the *payong* block to defend the opponent's slash strike.

Finish by countering with a slash to the opponent's jaw.

7 *Espada y Daga* – Sword and Dagger

History and Evolution

In the Philippines in the 1500s, a bladed weapon was likely to be expensive and owned only by tribal leaders or the Spanish Conquistadors. The most common weapon for the masses was more likely to be the fire-hardened stick. It is therefore likely to be a myth that Filipino martial arts were originally *only* blade-orientated, rather than blade *and* stick-orientated.

The Spanish conquerors brought their own European martial skills with them, particularly the fencing style of *espada y daga* (sword and dagger). From the late 1500s to the 1700s, Filipino blade fighting may have been influenced by Spanish fencing, and '*eskrima*' itself means 'fencing', from the Spanish *esgrima*. The extremely rare print shown below is from a book titled *The English Fencing Master or the Complete Tutor of the Small Sword* (1705). This depiction of the Spanish rapier and dagger technique is identical to a Filipino method called *Cruzada*.

Spanish Rapier and Dagger (1705).

The Spanish Raper and Dagger.

The Spanish tended to carry the dagger at the hip, *primarily* as a reserve or back-up weapon, preferring to keep the fight at long range (utilizing the very long length of the rapier), and occasionally using the dagger for defensive blocking or parrying. It appears that the Filipinos eventually modified this, bringing the knife forwards to hold just behind the sword. They were then able to use its manoeuvrability and deceptiveness as an extremely effective medium-range weapon.

Obviously, there is much greater risk in engaging an opponent with a sword at close range. However, when cautious Spanish conquerors removed or restricted the right to own or carry a bladed weapon, the Filipino warriors substituted with wooden sticks (at first, flattened to resemble a sword)

A rare photo of GM Fortunato 'Atong' Garcia demonstrating the use of the *daga* for thrusting at close range.

so they could continue training. This also breathed new life into the revival of the older native stick-fighting arts, which encouraged greater versatility and use of the left hand, and led to an increase in the type and variety of techniques and counters.

The late Grandmaster Filemon 'Momoy' Canete once told me that when he was studying the art from Grandmaster Doring Saavedra (in the 1920s), the *daga* was held near the hip and was used *primarily* as a reserve weapon, used mainly to parry the opponent's sword. It was only used for thrusting, when the opponent was almost 'finished' and the damage had been inflicted by the sword. This was because the favoured training weapon at the time was the *espada*. The characteristic sharp edge of this weapon dictated its use. It was very risky to engage an opponent at close range, hence the prevailing styles during this period were *larga mano* (long range) based. This has parallels with the Spanish method.

In the 1930s training with the 'live' *espada* fell out of vogue, probably due to the injuries it caused in training. A hardwood stick (sometimes flattened so as to maintain the characteristics of the sword) was substituted for the *espada*; the wooden dagger (*baraw*) was substituted for the metal *daga*.

In the 1940s, hardwood sticks began to be replaced with rattan sticks, called *olisi*, and this led to the development of a totally different system of stick and dagger. Due to the non-edged characteristic of the stick, disarming techniques were used liberally, and over time trapping and throwing techniques were incorporated. This method of using the stick and dagger became known as *olisi y baraw*.

According to Abner Pasa:

The passive role of the knife in the early period of the practice of espada y daga is understandable. The strategy adopted by fighters was practical and realistic. Since bladed weapons were used, it was considered very risky to move in close. The wider space afforded by medium range, and especially long range-based fighting styles, allowed the combatants more manoeuvrability and a longer reaction time.

However, with the growing popularity and wider acceptance of the use of the stick, the role of the knife changed drastically. It gained more prominence and importance. In fact, not only did it revolutionize the espada y daga system, but it also paved way for the development of the single stick system.

A problem of misinterpretation arises in modern times, when the methods of practising with one long weapon and one short weapon are generally referred to as *espada y daga*. This is somewhat misleading. The art effectively evolved in two directions, and although there is a certain amount of overlap, there are important distinctions between the two varieties:

Espada y daga: means sword and dagger. The techniques are more likely to start at long range, taking account of the character-istics of the sword, and only to bring in the use of the knife when a combination of initial defences and zoning (body movement towards a safer angle) makes it possible.

Olisi y baraw: means stick and dagger. There are snapping and curving techniques, which are appropriate to the use of a stick but would not be sensible with a sword. Furthermore, the 'stick and dagger' techniques make it possible to introduce a number of closer-range capturing, trapping, countering and disarming techniques, some of which would be foolish against a sword rather than a stick.

They are therefore two arts rather than one, but both types of training are excellent for developing body zoning, line familiarization and coordination. It just remains a funda-mental principle not to overlook the charac-teristics of the weapon.

Espada y daga (sword and dagger) is regarded by many old-time eskrimadors as the 'backbone' of the Filipino martial arts. Most of the old classical styles of Eskrima were *espada y daga* based. The reason for this

GM Orville Visitacion demonstrating the use of the *daga* for hand cutting at medium range.

GM Orville Visitacion uses the '*degaso*' technique to zone away from the opponent's *daga*.

was it rapidly developed footwork for zoning, and made the non-dominant hand 'come alive' by putting a dagger in it. This in turn developed better coordination.

Classical blade-orientated *espada y daga* is, therefore, long- to medium-range based, whilst *olisi y baraw*, which evolved much later, is medium- to close-range based.

Eventually the dagger hand became known as the 'live' hand or the 'third' hand – third, because the tip of the long weapon is the 'first hand', whilst the butt of the weapon is the 'second' hand. The line familiarization and constant monitoring of the *daga* hand led to the development of 'zoning' footwork.

Zoning means to be on the outside of one of the opponent's weapon arms: this is the safest place, as it 'zones' you away from the other arm.

Eventually these skills were adapted to empty hand combat, leading to the development of the very sophisticated *pangamut* system.

Espada y Daga Techniques

When I teach *espada y daga* techniques, I like to begin by separating the sword from the dagger. The first lesson with the sword is to understand its characteristics. Its

Edge-versus-edge contact (to be avoided).

Flat of the blade block-versus-edge contact.

Edge of the blade parry versus the flat of the blade.

'Inside' edge deflection versus the flat of the blade.

Daga supports espada (*fraile* method).

Daga used for a wrist cut.

cutting edge should not, under any circumstances, be used for blocking, as you run the risk of dulling your blade and may get it jammed.

The correct way to *block* with the sword is with the flat of the blade; use a 'fanning' motion to ensure the block is stable.

The edge of your sword can be used to *parry* the opponent's strike, but ensure that you strike the flat of your opponent's blade; once again avoid edge-to-edge contact.

The third way to use the sword is with the 'inside' edge: this part of the long blade is used to *deflect* the opponent's strike. A deflection requires better timing than a block, but its advantage is that it allows you to counter attack faster.

Once the basics of the sword have been covered, the next progression is to look at the different roles of the dagger. The use of the dagger is dependent on range: outside long range it can be used as a projectile, buying you time to close in. At long range, it is generally used as a reserve weapon for parrying. At medium range, the dagger can support the sword; this is done to reinforce the sword and helps to block strong blows: this type of method is called '*fraile*'.

From the fraile position, the dagger can be used to cut the opponent's wrist; however,

Daga used to trap the opponet's *espada* (*cruzada* method).

one should ensure that the opponent's dagger hand is 'monitored' at all times.

At medium range, the dagger can also be used to trap and redirect the opponent's sword; this type of method is called 'cruzada'.

At close range, the dagger can be used to disarm the opponent's sword. It is critical that the opponent's dagger is monitored at all times when disarming.

The final use of the dagger is for thrusting. It is critical that this is done from a zoned position, otherwise one runs the risk of a 'double kill'.

Daga used for disarming the opponent.

Daga used for thrusting.

The following sequence is an example of combining sword blocking, zoning foot-work, dagger thrusting and disarming.

On-guard position.

Blocking the slash attack and simultaneously cutting the opponent's hand.

Use the *punyo* of your espada to 'switch' to the zoned position, then follow up with a *daga* thrust.

Snake the opponent's *espada* and cut their wrist to dislodge the sword.

The sword is dislodged.

Move out of range of the *daga* thrust and chop the opponent's *daga* hand.

The *daga* is dislodged.

Finish with a *daga* thrust.

Olisi y Baraw Techniques

The following sequence, against a forehand slash, shows how to bind the opponent's stick, then hook the opponent's dagger, in turn trapping both arms. The stick is then used to off-balance the opponent for a takedown.

On-guard position.

Inside block and wrist cut.

Bind ('snake') the opponent's *olisi.*

Hook the opponent's *baraw* thrust.

The opponent's weapons are trapped.

The opponent is off balanced, and is ready to be taken down.

The final sequence exhibited is against a backhand slash: this time your stick binds the opponent's stick with a clockwise 'snaking' motion, and the *punyo* of your stick is then used to parry the opponent's dagger thrust. Once both of the opponents arms are trapped, you can counter with your own dagger thrust.

On-guard position.

Outside block and hand cut.

Bind the opponent's *olisi.*

Draw the opponent's *baraw* thrust.

Counter by hooking with the *olisi punyo.*

The opponent's weapons are trapped.

Finish with a *baraw* thrust.

Without the specific dangers of the sword, but with the awareness of the potential of the knife, it became possible to develop the *olisi y baraw* methods of using principles of trapping techniques (restricting the opponent's use of his limbs), and to combine this with refining line familiarization and the use of 'drawing' (creating an open line to encourage an attack, with the intention of having set up a counter-technique for dealing with it).

To the untrained eye, these training methods may seem strange. It is, after all, virtually impossible, outside a deliberately arranged and illegal duel, for two people to face each other in a practical situation armed with a knife and a stick each. However, looking at the principles involved, it is then easier to understand the advantages provided by such training. Two people having to train at close proximity with four weapons, two of them knives, developing a high degree of coordination and of awareness and openings, are developing just the kind of 'qualities' that will be useful in a real encounter, rather than practising a 'technique' they will find in a real encounter.

8 *Sibat* – Long Stick (Staff)

Styles and Systems

In the Western Visayas, such as Negros Occidental, the landscape is flatter and more open than some of the other Philippine islands. This type of terrain allows you to swing a long weapon without hindrance. As a result, the *sibat* (staff) or long stick as it is also known, is a popular weapon in this region, whereas in heavily wooded areas the short stick is more popular.

There are various staff systems in Negros, some of which are described below.

Taw-Taw
This method is believed to have evolved from the movements made with the fishing rod, popular among those fishing in the numerous creeks and rivers in the area. It favours the normal hold, and specializes in sliding strikes to the opponent's hands.

GM Rene Cornell demonstrates the power of the *tapado* strike.

GM Rene Cornell demonstrates the power of the *tapado*'s thrust.

Tuwang-Tuwang

This method was developed from the wooden pole, used to carry heavy objects that were balanced on one's shoulders. It is a close-in fighting system specializing in double-end striking, disarming and off-balancing.

Bugsay

This is a style popular amongst the coastal areas of Negros. It is based on the movements of the fisherman paddling his canoe called the '*banca*'. The style favours the reverse hold, and prefers parrying as opposed to blocking.

Tapado

Tapado is one of the better known long-stick methods. *Tapado* means 'You are finished', from the Hiligaynon word '*tapat*', which means 'finished'. It is an aggressive, attacking style characterized by simultaneous blocks and strikes. It favours blocking – 'meeting the force' – rather than parrying.

The photographs (*see* p. 123 and above) of the late Grandmaster René Cornell clearly demonstrates the raw power of the *tapado* system.

Lagas

Lagas means 'to pursue'. This style is one

ABOVE: GM Roqillio Espallago demonstrating a fluid *sciensa* movement.

BELOW: GM Roqillio Espallago demonstrating a *sciensa* thrusting technique.

of the older longer stick methods and is characterized by its forward pressure against an opponent. It does not advocate 'force to force' defence, and prefers to deflect and redirect the opponent's strikes.

Sciensa

Sciensa, meaning 'science', is a long stick method that emphasizes parrying as the primary method of defence. It is characterized by thrusting, and circular striking techniques.

The two photographs (*see* p. 125) of Grandmaster Roqillio Espallago clearly demonstrate the fluid circular and thrusting attacks found in the *sciensa* system.

Measurement

The length of the staff advocated by various styles varies, but essentially it falls into three heights: ground to sternum, ground to chin and ground to eyebrow.

Holds and Grips

Different long-stick methods prefer different methods of holding the staff. Essentially there are three types of hold: normal hold, reverse hold and centre hold.

The grip used when holding the staff falls into two categories, these being a fixed grip or fluid grip. A fixed grip will maintain the same hold, whilst a fluid grip will shift from one hold to another.

Numerada

The following twelve-count striking template is from the *sciensa* method, developed by the late Grandmaster Fortunato 'Atong' Garcia. I like this template because it encompasses a wide variety of strikes, and the sequence is such that each strike flows seamlessly into the next. It should be practised in the three types of hold, and with both a fixed and fluid grip. The targets are as described in the following *numerada* illustration.

Normal hold.

Reverse hold.

Centre hold.

Staff *numerada*.

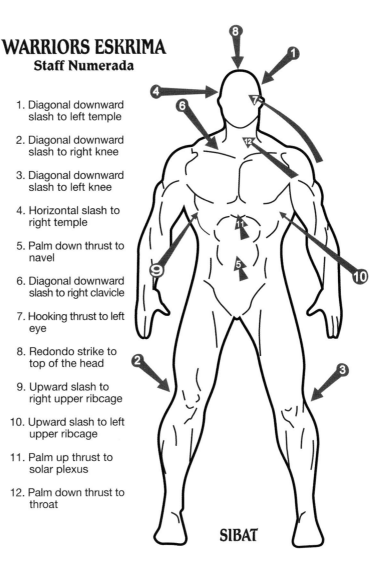

WARRIORS ESKRIMA
Staff Numerada

1. Diagonal downward slash to left temple

2. Diagonal downward slash to right knee

3. Diagonal downward slash to left knee

4. Horizontal slash to right temple

5. Palm down thrust to navel

6. Diagonal downward slash to right clavicle

7. Hooking thrust to left eye

8. Redondo strike to top of the head

9. Upward slash to right upper ribcage

10. Upward slash to left upper ribcage

11. Palm up thrust to solar plexus

12. Palm down thrust to throat

SIBAT

Defences

Generally speaking, the various long-stick systems will defend an opponent's strikes in two basic ways. These are blocking and parrying.

Blocking: This type of defence involves intercepting an opponent's strike before it can gather full momentum; the block must be secure as you are 'meeting' the opponent's force.

Parrying: This type of defence 'follows' the opponent's strike; it requires better timing to apply effectively, but has the advantage of leaving the opponent more vulnerable to your counter attack.

Counter Attacks

The following four sequences show four different defences, and counter attacks against a forehand slash.

Tapado: The following sequence is a typical *tapado* response against a forehand slash attack. Note how the block drives the opponent's staff towards the ground, leaving him open to the upward eye thrust; if the opponent evades the eye thrust by leaning back, his hands are still vulnerable to a disabling downward strike.

Bugsay: Since the *bugsay* method holds the long stick in a reverse hold, it can 'scoop' the opponent's strike in a counter-clockwise direction, and counter with a sliding strike to the opponent's hand.

On-guard position.

Block opponent's slash and drive opponent's staff to the ground.

Counter with an upward thrust to the eye.

Finish with a hand smash.

On-guard position.

Defend the opponent's strike with a counter-clockwise parry (beginning).

Counter-clockwise parry (completion).

Sciensa: As can be seen from the on-guard position, the staff is chambered to parry the opponent's strike; note how the 'point' of the staff faces the opponent after the parry is completed, which allows you to rapidly counter with a 'gouging' thrust to the eyes, and finish with a circular downward hand smash.

Counter attack with upward groin strike.

Tuwang-Tuwang: Since the *tuwang-tuwang* system adopts a centre hold, it can use the centre of the staff to intercept the opponent's strike, and the outer end of the staff can then hook the opponent's weapon and disarm it; a finishing strike to the throat is an effective follow-up.

On-guard position.

Parry the opponent's strike.

Thrust to eye.

Chamber for arm smash.

Downward strike to forearm.

On-guard position.

Jam the opponent's strike and block with the centre of your staff.

Hook the opponent's staff in a counter-clockwise direction.

Start to dislodge the staff (beginning).

Dislodging the staff is achieved.

Flow Drills

Sombrada

The *sombrada* flow drill, exhibited in the double sticks chapter, can also be done with the single stick, the stick and dagger, and the staff. The flow drill can allow both individuals to block and counter, in a 'one-for-one' manner. The defences and strikes remain the same; the only difference with the staff is that *both* of your hands are gripping the weapon at the same time. This has an added benefit in that both right and left arms are being trained; training with a staff also emphasizes body mechanics. Since the staff is a much heavier weapon, you cannot rely on swinging it with the arm only, and the *whole* of the body (arms, torso, hips and legs) will have to come into play.

Sparring

Sparring with staffs should always be done with protective gear. The awesome power that the staff can generate greatly increases the chances of injury, so a head guard, body protector, elbow pads, forearm guards, hand gloves, groin guard and knee pads are essential. Start with 50 per cent power and progressively increase the intensity.

Finish with a strike to the throat.

9 Flexible Weapons

The *latigo* forms part of the flexible weapons category of Eskrima; this category also includes the *cadena* (chain), *tabak tayuk* (also spelt *tabak tayok* (*nunchaku*)), and the *malong* (sash), also known as the *sarong* in Mindanao.

Whip (*Latigo*)

The whip was originally used as a herding tool, according to Yale history professor and historian William Henry Scott; the Filipino tribesmen were recognized by the invading Spanish forces as exceptional cattle herders in their initial interactions.

The whip's chief advantage is its ability to keep an opponent at a safe distance; its focused power when cracked has devastatingly high impact characteristics. In addition its flexible characteristics give it close-range options for binding and choking opponents. The handle of the whip can also be used as both a flexible and an impact weapon.

In the Philippines there are generally two types of whip: the bull whip and the horse whip. The bull whip, which is the longer in length, is usually made out of *abaca* rope, while the horse whip is usually made out of leather. The horse whip has a faster action and permits more multiple hits, whilst the bull whip is the more powerful of the two.

Traditional Filipino bull whip.

Normal grip.

A rare photo of GM Pasa cracking the whip, while GM Momoy Canete observes from the background.

Three-quarter grip.

Binding grip.

The whip used for trapping; note how the handle is lined up for striking.

For combat purposes, items such as fish hooks, barbed wire, ball bearings and broken glass could be attached to the distal end, to ensure maximum damage to the opponent.

One of Grandmaster Abner Pasa's training methods used to develop accuracy, spatial awareness and correct distance with the whip was to cut leaves hanging from branches. The goal was to choose a leaf and progressively cut a layer off it without disturbing any of the other leafs on the branch.

There are three basic whip grips: the normal grip, the three-quarter grip and the binding grip. The normal grip is used primarily for cracking the whip, in order to keep the opponent at a distance.

The three-quarter grip is used for close-quarter whipping, and the handle is also used as a flexible striking weapon.

The binding grip is used for trapping the opponent's arms, choking and takedowns.

The whip is also used as a cross-training tool, to develop the correct body mechanics that enhance other aspects of Eskrima. For example, training with the whip will certainly enhance the focus and power of one's single-stick *witik* strikes. *Witik* strikes are wrist-orientated and require a strong whipping action to generate power.

Training with the whip will also improve your projectile technique, particularly when deploying a 'light' projectile such as a pen, pencil or chopstick. The relaxation, acceleration and focus of power developed with the whip will add the strength required to effectively deploy a light projectile.

The *Malong*

The *malong* is a traditional sash that can be worn around the waist or across the torso; from a non-combative perspective, it can be used as a shopping bag, for example, or a table cloth. From a combative viewpoint it can be used as a flexible weapon or for close-quarter tactics, such as chokes and strangles.

The following sequence shows how the *malong* can be used to counter an opponent attempting a double leg takedown. Note how the left hand is used to offset the opponent's tackle, and how the right hand feeds the *malong* around the opponent's neck.

On-guard position.

The opponent attempts a takedown: jam with your left arm.

Wrap the *malong* around the opponent's neck.

Pull the head down and apply a choke hold.

The Scarf

Since the *malong* is not part of most people's attire in the UK, the scarf becomes an effective alternative. It can be efficiently removed from the neck and used as a flexible weapon, or it can be used to parry the opponent's attack, and counter with close-range tactics such as disarming.

On-guard position.

Tabak Tayuk/Cadena

The *tabak tayuk*, more popularly known as the *nunchaku*, and the *cadena* (chain), are also part of Eskrima's flexible weapons category. They require a high level of skill and spatial awareness to wield effectively, and are generally taught at a more advanced level of Eskrima. They are therefore beyond the scope of this book.

Use a scarf as a flexible weapon.

Use a scarf to parry a knife thrust.

Counter with a disarming tactic.

Tabak tayuk and *cadena*.

10 Projectiles

Projectiles have been part of the Filipino combat arts since the earliest times. Archaeological evidence from burial jars found in the cave cemeteries known as the Tabon Caves (island of Palawan) show bronze and iron artefacts that date back to 200 BC. Among the items found were arrowheads. Apart from deploying arrows, the Filipinos were adept at using the blowgun with poisoned arrows, and at throwing axes.

From the viewpoint of self-defence, instilling an awareness of the use of projectiles is possibly the most neglected aspect of martial arts training. Self-defence is normally taught on the basis of an alternative between avoidance and physical conflict. You are taught that either you can avoid physical conflict altogether (whether through the use of psychology to negotiate or defuse a situation, or simply through physical escape such as by running away), or that you need to acquire methods to use when engaging in direct contact with the attacker(s) (whether by striking, unbalancing, locking).

In between these situations is the use of projectiles. There may very well be a situation where there is enough distance between you and the threat for you not to have to either hit or be hit, but where the threat is difficult to avoid or escape unless you can cause distraction or pain while you effect an escape.

There may also very well be a situation in which you are not yet at touching distance, but feel that it is inevitable; and you also feel that once you are physically engaged, the apparent size or strength of the attacker would give them a serious advantage over you. However, if you have something that can be thrown at them first, this may just make it possible for you to do something else to them while they are distracted by reacting to what has been thrown – it could make the difference between being cornered, and having a chance to unbalance them in one direction while you make a rapid escape in the other.

The first principle, therefore, is simply the awareness of the concept of projectiles. The word 'projectiles' is not being used in any formal or 'classical' way here, in the sense of referring to javelins or throwing knives or axes and suchlike. It is used to mean absolutely anything that can be thrown at an opponent, including coins, pens, pencils, a bag, a bunch of keys, a jacket, or indeed anything within reach, depending on your situation.

Let us take an example. If you were sitting at a table in a restaurant and you were unfortunate enough to have your meal interrupted by an aggressor with a blunt or edged weapon, looking for a victim to attack, your awareness of projectiles could change the situation drastically. Obviously each situation is different, and you have to make judgements on the spot that will not cause you to recklessly endanger any other innocent persons present.

However, you would at least initially be outside the range of direct physical contact, and you would be surrounded by potential projectiles: cutlery, plates, cups, sauce bottles, salt and pepper shakers. If it were safe (to others) to do so, you could cause this potential attacker an astounding amount of distraction and irritation by bombarding him with such items, possibly enabling him to be overcome (by you or others) or even causing him to retreat, rather than him remaining focused on his original intentions. Nevertheless, always endeavour to adhere to your country's law regarding the use of reasonable force (*see* Chapter 13)

Without the fundamental awareness of projectiles as your first range of attack (outside physical contact range), such an 'interpretation' of the potential use of your surroundings would not even occur to you. But with the awareness of using many items as projectiles, it can be difficult to imagine a situation in which you are ever completely 'unarmed'!

Once you have such *awareness* of the concept, however, the next principle is the development of projectile *skills*. Using throwing knives, for example, is not about encouraging any law-abiding citizen to carry throwing knives during their daily life. Having an increased ability to judge the distance to the target, the weight of the item being thrown, and to hit more specific targets (rather than just throwing in a general direction) can only make the use of such a concept more accurate, deliberate and effective in a practical situation.

Most civilians during their day-to-day activities will have access to coins, pens or pencils. It therefore makes sense to practise throwing these types of item. The way the projectile is thrown will depend on where it is carried; this could be the trouser pocket, or the shirt pocket.

Chopstick Evasion Drill

The following drill is an excellent training method for sharpening one's reflexes, and also learning how to effectively deploy projectiles. For illustrative purposes, wooden chopsticks are used. When practising any kind of projectile training, always wear eye protection, as there is a risk of the projectile rebounding towards your face.

In the following example, the chopstick is deployed from the trouser pocket; the defender should try to evade the projectile with footwork, head movement or use the stick to deflect the projectile.

Detailed projectile training is beyond the scope of this book, but hopefully this introductory chapter has given you an insight into this lesser known aspect of Eskrima, and will motivate you to research it further.

The correct grip for throwing a light projectile.

Always wear eye protection.

The projectile is drawn from the attacker's pocket.

Ready to deploy.

The projectile is deployed (note it is aimed at the person's glasses).

The projectile is deflected.

11 Solo Training and Training with Equipment

Karenza

Eskrima is an energy-based art; to really experience its essence you need to have a stimulus. Receiving and feeding energy to your *guro* (instructor) or training partner is the ideal. However, quite often one has to train alone, due to reasons of location, varying levels of commitment amongst individuals, and so on. *Karenza* (shadowfighting), if performed correctly, is perhaps the best solo training method. The key to performing *karenza* correctly is developing effective visualization skills. The eskrimador when performing karenza should visualize fighting against different types of opponent; these could be long-, medium- or close-range stylists.

The long-range fighter likes to use their reach to the maximum; in weapons combat this usually means that the hands and legs will be the primary targets. In an empty hand context, straight kicks or straight punching will be the favoured tools. Typically, this type of fighter will use a lot of footwork to move in and out of range.

The medium-range stylist likes to crash in and stand his ground. 'Crashing' is a term used to describe closing the gap from long to medium range, and is usually accomplished with some kind of block – the roof block is a popular choice amongst this type of stick fighter. Once inside, strikes to the head and torso are preferred. From an empty hands perspective, this type of fighter usually prefers to use medium-range tools such as hook punches and knee strikes.

The close-range stick fighter will use a lot of *punyos* (butt strikes), *witiks* (wrist flicks) or non-linear strikes. The checking hand will also be used more extensively (than at medium range) to control the opponent's weapon hand. In empty hands, tools such as the uppercut, elbows and head butts would be employed effectively.

Once you can visualize the above, you can work on counter tactics and strategies to fight such opponents. This will keep your *karenza* realistic, and allow you to transfer your skill sets to partner application.

You can apply other types of 'theme' when practising *karenza*; for example, visualize an opponent who is a counter fighter – someone who will not lead and bring the attack to you. As a result, proficiency in baiting or feinting is required in order to draw his attack. Therefore, one theme could be to start every attack with a fake. Remember, the difference between a fake and a real attack is that the fake does not make contact. It should 'look' like a real attack, however, and this involves much practice. Realistic feinting is an advanced part of Eskrima that few people master.

Another theme could be power strikes only. This would be practising an attacking theme to overwhelm an opponent, who perhaps has a weak defence. However, the danger of power striking only is that you may restrict the flow and rely on singular focused strikes. As a result, to stay well rounded and

Darren Moore practising *karenza*.

A final theme would be to visualize fighting multiple opponents. This is an excellent theme for developing footwork and awareness: a risk of shadow-fighting is to stand in one spot and strike from there – but if you visualize you are fighting two or three opponents you will have to move, and this naturally promotes footwork.

Two hallmarks of Eskrima are creativity and flexibility, and theming the *karenza* will get you to think creatively and remain a flexible eskrimador, thus becoming someone who can adapt to any opponent or style.

Training Equipment

Eskrima in the Philippines developed in an economy of scarcity. This led to the development of unique training equipment, ingenuity of mind being the key.

Tyres – Eskrima's Heavy Bag

When one thinks of training apparatus used for developing power in striking, the heavy punchbag comes to mind. In the Philippines, traditionally car tyres were substituted for this. The tyre could be single and hanging from a tree, it could be a stack of tyres over a fencing post, rubber strips nailed to a post, or half a tyre attached to a post.

The purpose of striking tyres is to condition the hands, develop grip and increase the power of one's strikes. The limitation of only striking in the air is that you don't get any kinaesthetic feedback, whereas when you strike the tyres, you will get kinaesthetic feedback. To begin with, the hands will blister, however, persevere, and in time the hands will become conditioned. When you strike the tyres, if the hand is not aligned correctly, you will feel the strain on your wrist, and/or you will disarm yourself. With practice however, your grip will become more secure.

A strike, whether it is with a stick or the empty hands, should not travel at a uniform rate; rather, it should gather speed (accelera-

not predictable, another theme could be that there must be a minimum of four strikes thrown. This will develop combination striking and flow.

A danger of shadow-fighting is that one can become too attack-orientated, with no simulation of defensive skills. A good theme to limit this would be to finish every combination with a defensive move – for example, return to an on-guard position, move out of range, block. Becoming too reliant on one grip or becoming right side dominant is another danger, therefore, a theme of switching hands and grips during the round of shadow-fighting is highly recommended. Hand- and grip-switching makes you unorthodox and hard to read.

GM Pasa striking the tyre post.

tion) and finish with a snap. The key to acceleration is relaxation: the arm must remain relaxed until the last few inches of the strike. Proper body mechanics is the key to increasing the power of one's strikes, and some eskrimadors never realize their true striking potential due to faulty body mechanics.

One of my teachers used to say, 'Punch with your feet and kick with your hands, use your body as one unit!' This insight helped me understand that power originates from the ground, that it travels through the leg drive, is picked up by the whip of the torso, transferred to the shoulder, and finally transmitted through the arm. Upon impact, the

PG Godhania
striking the three
ball contraption.

strike should feel like a whiplash. This is one of the major benefits of training with a whip or flexible weapon: it develops relaxation and proper body mechanics.

When striking the tyres with sticks, aim to hit with the tip of the stick; this is what is travelling at the highest speed and will have the most impact. Striking with the middle of the stick will have 50 per cent less impact than the tip. Avoid gripping the stick too tightly: a secure grip with the middle and ring finger is sufficient – the other fingers can tighten upon impact with the tyre. This will keep your arm relaxed, and is one of the key components of hitting hard.

Dion Trigg training on the hanging stick.

The Three Ball Contraption

The three ball contraption is to Eskrima what the top and bottom ball is to Western boxing. The balls used for this contraption are usually golf balls, because they are durable and present a small target. The balls are positioned at three heights: the head, hands, and knee level. One bungee cord attaches the device to a hook towards the ceiling, and another attaches the device to a hook on the floor. This training aid, designed by Grandmaster Abner Pasa, is excellent for improving one's hand/eye coordination, accuracy and timing.

To use the device, you pull the bungee cord so that you are presented with a moving target. The movement can be from side to side, or forwards and back. If you fixate on the targets, they will be difficult to hit, instead look to the side so that you can use your peripheral vision, this will make it considerably easier to strike the golf balls. The accuracy of your strikes will be easily discerned, as you will get auditory feedback from the sound of the stick hitting the golf ball. Through practice, you will develop the correct timing to strike accurately.

When using this training device, don't be limited to the single stick. Practise using the double sticks, *olisi y baraw*, knife and staff. Don't go for power hitting, but work on combination striking, with the emphasis on flow and accuracy.

The Hanging Stick

Eskrima's hanging stick device is the ideal

Dion Trigg training on the thrusting ball.

training tool for developing reflexes and quick reactions. As the name suggests, it is simply a stick, tied in the middle and hung from a hook. The real value of this training aid is that it presents erratic movement when hit; this makes it a challenge to react to. When you strike one end of the stick, it will spin and the other end will come towards your head quickly. Be ready to block, duck or move out of range, and whichever response you choose will have to be made in a split second; over time your reactions will improve tremendously.

The limitation of many training apparatus is that they are mainly designed to develop offensive skills; this can lead to a neglect of recovery after striking and the use of defensive movements. The hanging stick gives you immediate feedback by attacking you after you have struck it, this will force you to recover with some kind of defensive movement.

The Thrusting Ball

The thrusting ball, as the name suggests, is designed for isolating and perfecting thrusting techniques. The ball is made from rattan skin, and is woven in such a way that there are small gaps for the stick to thrust through. The ball is hung and once moving presents a small target. As a training aid its primary purpose is to develop accuracy and timing of the thrust.

According to Grandmaster Pasa:

The thrust is the most underestimated strike of the stick. The very small point presented by the stick appears less threatening than it really is. However, the small point actually allows the greatest concentration of power that can be focused in any strike. The speed of delivery of the strike is phenomenal. This type of strike is most effective when directed against vital points in the body such as the eyes, throat, solar plexus, groin etc. In temperate countries where people usually wear heavy clothing which can act as body protection, thrusting techniques would be most appropriate.

Coconut Breaking

Coconuts are difficult to break; some martial artists temper their hands and practise breaking them with the bare hands. In Eskrima, the stick is used to break the coconut. The purpose of the exercise is to develop the focus of the mind, and test the effectiveness of your technique – but remember this: no matter how sound the technique is mechanically, its effectiveness will depend on the following factors:

- The speed with which it is delivered.
- The force that generates the strike.
- The accuracy on the target area.
- The timing of the strike.
- Correct judgement of distance between you and the target.
- The acceleration of the strike.
- The level of relaxation present throughout the movement.

Coconuts give you visual feedback, and a successful break 'aims to draw the water out'. Training with the tyres is recommended prior to attempting coconut breaks, as a prerequisite would be a solid grip and strength in the wrist. There are three levels of coconut breaking: in the first the coconut is secured in some kind of vice; in the second it is put inside some netting, secured from the top but allowed to move freely from the bottom; and in the third it is thrown and must be broken in mid-flight.

The type of strike used to break the coconut will also determine the difficulty of the break. Strikes such as slashes and *redondos* 'follow through' the target, whereas *witik* strikes such as *abanikos* or *curvada*, aka 'snapping' strikes, do not follow through but retract upon impact. Therefore, they are more akin to a whip strike. It is considerably more difficult to break the coconut with *witik* strikes, as you have a shorter distance to generate the force required to achieve the break. Considerable training is required to achieve the level of wrist flexibility and grip strength required to make *witik* strikes very powerful.

The Banana Tree

The trunk of a banana tree is used in Eskrima for projectile training, live blade cutting, and empty hands/legs conditioning. The fibres of the banana tree are such that they 'give' when struck with the empty hands, which gives it the feeling of a human body. It is also easy to stick projectiles into the tree, and there is minimal worry of the object rebounding back towards your face – this is the major safety concern when throwing projectiles. Similar to the Japanese sword arts, where straw is used to practise live blade cutting, some eskrimadors use the banana tree. The tree does not damage your blade, and gives you realistic feedback. Sometimes you will achieve a clean cut, and sometimes the blade will get stuck, and you will learn ways of how to free the blade.

The late Grand Master 'Ingko Yoling' Canete used to tell a story about Pablo Alicante, a famous and feared eskrimador from Toledo City, Cebu. A challenge match had been arranged between Alicante and the unbeaten Doring Saavedra. Yoling on behalf of Saavedra went to 'check out' Alicante prior to the fight. Alicante took Yoling to a place where there were some banana trees, and then asked him to 'choose one'. Alicante then proceeded to fell the tree with one strike with his *kamagong* stick!

ABOVE: PG Godhania coconut breaking, under GM Pasa's watchful eye.

BELOW: PG Godhania throwing nails into the banana tree.

12 Eskrima Philosophy

by Abner Pasa

There are two powers in the world, the sword and the mind.
In the long run, the sword is always beaten by the mind.

Napoleon Bonaparte

The weapon of the warrior is the mind; the implement in the hand is just a tool, which is an extension of the mind. Hence the importance of strategy over technique. This foregoing statement reflects the insight gained over all the years I have spent studying and researching the Filipino martial arts. It is of some comfort to know that Musashi shares the same thoughts, as expressed in his book, *A Book of Five Rings* – that 'Strategy is the craft of the warrior'. He elaborated that: 'The warrior's is the twofold way of pen and sword' (1974: 37).

Is there a 'Filipino martial art'? What is it? What is its philosophy? The answer to the first question is 'yes' and 'no'. There is a martial art distinctly Filipino, but it is still evolving.

Each group of people has its own way of combat, and the Filipino combat system is no different. It is a system of fighting that is only concerned with the complete annihilation of the opponent. But is it a martial art? In becoming a 'martial art' (the blending of martial or a warlike activity with art indicating something aesthetic) one uses its combative traditions, but instead of seeking to crush the opponent it now views him as a partner in the process of knowing his 'self'.

Thus, based upon Thomas Cleary's translation of Sun-Tzu's point of view of fighting in the book, *Mastering the Art of War* (1989), it is true that to win without fighting is best. Sun-Tzu also posited that when contention escalates to conflict, there is already a loss even in victory, and this can lead to even greater loss even after it has ended. In addition, we might accept Raymond S. Stites' definition of art in his book, *Arts and Man* (1940:13):

Art (is) the most direct language of the soul, and the means by which man completely unifies his emotional and intellectual life so that his feelings as well as his thoughts can be transmitted to others. Yet art is more than communication. Through artistic creation and enjoyment – whether in the field of literature, sculpture or music – man becomes succinctly aware of his oneness with nature and his fellow man.

With this lofty definition of what an art is, even a martial one, then we can conclude that there is still no Filipino martial art. Rather, there are different styles of predominantly stick fighting forms currently being taught as fighting systems in the Philippines. As with the Japanese fighting systems that transformed their combative systems (*jutsu*) into martial arts (*do*), there is an evolving combative system that is seeking to transform the traditional purely *fighting* styles into a more socially acceptable and modern form as a *martial* art.

What makes it Filipino is its uniqueness. It is a weapons-based system. That is, it is training using weapons from the beginning, with any empty-hand abilities a consequence of its weapons training, because training against a hand is inconsequential after training against weapons. This unique quality of Filipino systems may be explained by the commentary of Karl Jaspers in his book: *The Origin and Goal of History* (1953: 36). He noted that:

Every animal, without exception, develops organs adapted to particular tasks in connexion with the special circumstance obtaining in the particular environment by which its life is confined. This specialization of organs results in every animal being superior to man at some point, in terms of particular abilities. But this very superiority means, at the same time, a narrowing down of its potentialities. Man has avoided all such specializations of his organs. Hence the fact that though he is inferior in each individual organ, he remains superior in the potentialities he has kept alive by non-specialization. He is compelled by his inferiority and enabled by his superiority, through the medium of his consciousness, to follow paths quite different from those taken by animals in bringing his existence to realization. It is this, and not his body, that renders him capable of adapting himself to all climates and all zones, to all situations and all environments.... Thanks to the absence of organ specialization, he remained open to possibilities for the fashioning of his environment, in which his organs were replaced by implements.

Furthermore, the term 'Filipino' has a rather interesting history. According to William Henry Scott in his book, *Barangay: Sixteenth Century Philippine Culture and Society* (1994: 6-7), in 1542 Ruy Lopez de Villalobos named the islands of Leyte and Samar, *Filipinas* after the young prince who would become King Philip II, from which the later colony would be called *Las Islas Filipinas*. The Spaniards called the natives of the archipelago *indios*, compounding Christopher Columbus's well known error, when he thought he had reached the Orient – that is, the Indies – in the Caribbean. However, when it was necessary to distinguish the *indios* of the Philippines from those of the Americas, they were called Filipinos.

In the nineteenth century, Spaniards born in the colony began to be known as *Espanoles filipino* to distinguish them from Spaniards born in Spain, a designation that was logically contracted to *Filipinos* when speaking of Spaniards. Philippine-born Spaniards, however, often resented being called Filipinos by *peninsulares*, preferring the term *hijos del pais* – children of the land.

When American invaders seized the Spanish colony as spoils of the Spanish–American War, they called its inhabitants Filipinos, and so today citizens of the Republic of the Philippines are recognized in international law as Filipinos.

The second part of the query is whether the Filipino fighting style developed its own unique philosophy. What is philosophy? The word comes from two Greek words *philein*, which means 'to love,' and *Sophia*, meaning 'knowledge' or 'wisdom'. The term, for purposes of my advocated philosophical notion, means a seeker of knowledge. I agree absolutely with the observation of Brooke Noel Moore and Kenneth Bruder in their book, *Philosophy: The Power of Ideas* (1990: 3) that 'anytime we think or talk about a topic long enough, provided thatour thinking or discourse is organized, we very well have engaged in philosophy.' Thus, perhaps not well stated, just as Filipino fighting styles are evolving as a martial art, so too, there is a philosophy that is evolving as well.

In an effort to create a '*do*', or way, as well as develop a philosophical foundation to the evolving Filipino martial art, I have developed the following fundamental principles, which are used in the practice of a Filipino martial art in the Warriors system. These principles are recognized as the most primitive components of various different styles and practices I have been trained in. The following eight principles will hopefully serve as a framework in an effort to bring together divergent styles that exist in the country today. These fundamental principles, arranged in alphabetical order, are:

- The Appropriateness Principle.
- The Awareness Principle.
- The Balance Principle.
- The Characteristic of Tool Principle.
- The Nature of Environment Principle.
- The Objectiveness Principle.
- The Skilfulness Principle.
- The Universality Principle.

Below, I have further arranged the principles into sub groups, which provide a connective foundation.

Skills Acquisition Triad

Study and training in the Filipino martial arts is essentially aimed at developing skills necessary to survive life-threatening situations. The skills acquisition triad involved in developing and mastering skills includes the Characteristic of Tool Principle, the Nature of Environment Principle and the Balance Principle. These three need to be taken together in their proper combination to achieve optimal effectiveness and efficiency.

The orientation of training is essentially of a defensive nature. Atong Garcia was a self-confessed illiterate (he missed schooling because his '*lolo*' demanded his company, arguing that the '*carabao*' never went to school but was strong and doing well), whom I found to be one of the best stick fighters I have had the chance to play against, and a man of profound practical wisdom. Atong Garcia stressed the defensive point by using a child as an example. He said

that a child, even without training, when given a stick will know how to use it and hit someone who threatens him, but if he is attacked he would be hard pressed to defend himself properly if he is not taught how to do it. Therefore Tio Atong, as he was often fondly called, insists that training should be primarily of a defensive posture – to defend oneself against attacks.

In Warriors Eskrima the notion of defence is very simple: we use the principle of 'hiding behind the stick'. This means that even if your stick is only an inch thick, if you are able to put it between you and the opponent every time he attacks, then you may as well be hiding behind a wall. A very simple idea, although a bit difficult to execute in practice, and one needs to train diligently over a long period of time. The essential element of this skill is timing. An example of using the strategy of hiding behind the stick is to use the *wiper* – so called because the movement is executed by simply mimicking the movement of the windshield wiper in the car – and its inverse form the *pendulum*.

These patterns, shown on p. 151, were recognized during the process of isolating movements within techniques being taught using the new science of biomechanics. My training was essentially a simple approach of just doing it. In a way, it was the method of learning the 'school of hard knocks' approach. In the language of the Warriors Eskrima, a philosophy that states that 'man can only *think* and *act*', the process of learning was through the capacity of man to act. The thinking part was what came after, when I was already involved in the task of teaching others.

To facilitate the teaching process, a verbalization of what I had learned to do was necessary. It has been my experience that in teaching a movement, demonstration or 'showing' is the better and more effective way of facilitating learning by the students. A graphic illustration of the 'wiper' notion is shown above.

GM Garcia – 'wiper' defence.

Defence for attacks to the lower part of the body is dealt with in the 'inverse drill', and will not be discussed here due to space limitation. This exercise is very useful in long-range engagement.

The Characteristic of Tool Principle

This principle addresses the question of 'What?': that is, to what end is the tool to be used? Aristotle noted that a special-purpose tool is more effective when used for the particular task it is designed for, but a general purpose tool is more practical and convenient to meet contingencies existing in practical situations. One cannot possibly carry a special tool for all anticipated needs. So one compromises and settles for a general purpose tool to serve as many possible scenarios as possible, then relies on one's creativity to

The wiper concept of defence is made by keeping your hand holding the stick stationary (preferably in the middle of your body) and using the tip of the stick to swing to and fro from left to right, and vice versa to meet blows coming from the left or the right. This stratagem works best at close range and offers protection for attacks to the upper part of the body, especially blows directed to the head.

Shown opposite is an illustration of the pendulum concept of defence. Its pattern is the opposite of the wiper, in the sense that instead of using the hand holding the stick as the base (the fulcrum, if we look at the movement as a lever), you utilize the tip of the stick as the base. Then you swing your hand holding the stick to-and-from left to right and vice versa to meet blows coming from your left or right. This works best in medium range and to a limited extent in close range, for attacks directed to the middle part of the body.

GM Garcia – 'pendulum' defence.

work around the limits of tools available under the circumstances. This condition promoted the development of the two main characteristics of a Filipino fighter: a very high sense of *flexibility* and *creativity*.

Some anthropologists posit that man, lacking the fang and the claw, must necessarily be a club-wielding animal. The primitive weapons of man were the stone and the stick, and these primitive weapons have somehow become the mainstay for the Filipino martial artist. The most convenient and readily available implement in nature is the stick. It seems that the Filipino fighter has stayed closer to his ancient primitive roots by choosing to use a stick in combat situations.

The Nature of Environment Principle

This principle addresses the question of 'Where?' That is, under what conditions is the tool going to be used? The Nature of Environment principle considers the limits and possibilities of the tool or implement in relation with the physical circumstances. For example, a long weapon would be more appropriate if one were fighting in an open field, but when forced to fight in tight places the long weapon would be difficult if not impossible to use.

Balance Principle

This principle addresses the question of 'How?' That is, how will one ensure the choice of technique to be used to deal with a particular setting achieve the desired result that it is effective, and which works?

The fighter must be cognizant of the limits and possibilities of the twin forces Characteristic of the Tool and the Nature of Environment working together to achieve optimal performance in dealing with threats, thus ensuring one's survival. This principle implies the fact that there are no special techniques, or silver bullets – that nothing is absolute. Therefore, in using the triad princi-

ple, one needs to harmonize the nature of both principles. One must realize that in this world of ours everything is in constant flux – change. It is timely to note Thomas Cleary (1989:1) who said in *The Book of Balance and Harmony* that: 'Change and movement have their times; safety and danger are in oneself. . . . For those who master change, even disturbance is orderly.' Balance and harmony must be achieved in life. In the language of another era and in another culture, this advice can be equated to Socrates' admonition that our goal in life is to 'know thyself'.

The term 'balance' does not refer to a posture. It is an appreciation or an attitude of being open to the situation, thus allowing one to exercise an act of judgment that possesses the quality of adaptation between the qualities of the tool and the ground upon which it is used to gain optimal results.

With the above triad, the next principles become applicable.

The Awareness Principle

This principle promotes a proactive attitude towards life, a commitment to live life to the full, whatever your limits may be – by being 'alive,' this was borne out of an incident while training in the Excalibur system. Being one of the senior students I was approached by a student who asked, 'What will you do when two '*sanggot*' (scythes) are placed on your neck?' I was surprised with the question and replied, 'How was he able to do that in the first place?' This eventually allowed me to formulate this principle. The point is that one can minimize risks if one is vigilant and keenly aware of one's surroundings.

The Warriors Eskrima recognizes four sources of aggression or violence, and these are called the four S's of aggression: superiority in number, superiority in strength, superiority in skills or weapons, and surprise. Therefore, by simply being constantly aware of your surroundings, you can reduce, if not eliminate, the possibility of being surprised or caught unawares, thus reducing risks and enhancing the chances of survival in a harsh environment.

The Objectiveness Principle

In his book, *Questioning Krishnamurti* (1996), J. Krishnamurti insisted that everyone is conditioned by their culture, by their experiences, by their series of beliefs. Therefore all of us, being conditioned in that behavioural pattern, are biased in one way or the other. Consequently, our appreciation of anything will always be tainted by that bias. It does not take much to realize that this bias would be a serious weakness in a crisis situation, where decisions need to be made not only with split-second timing but also correctly.

In my career I have noted that we achieve better results if we adopt an attitude of objectivity. The life we live is dictated by the choices we make, therefore, it is imperative that we verify our premises and ensure that our facts are unbiased. Here, we take the prudent advice of Marie-Dominique Philippe, elucidated in his book, *Retracing Reality* (1999), to respect the limitation of our language and experience, to represent the fullness of the reality as such. Therefore, it is imperative that we always go back to the reality to verify our judgments.

Consequently our life and how we live it are simplified and made more fruitful, and costly mistakes, errors and faults are thus avoided. In life-threatening situations our chances of survival are improved.

Twin Horns Paradigm

The approach towards skills acquisition and its use is guided by the Skilfulness Principle and the Appropriateness Principle. In training, the Skilfulness Principle prevails, but in the application of those skills the Appropriateness Principle gains dominance. These two principles are called the Twin Horns Paradigm, and guide a student to greater levels of effectiveness, efficiency and adaptation, which characterize the quality of a master in the art.

The Skilfulness Principle

The main characteristic of skilfulness is the ability to perform effective techniques in the most efficient manner. Therefore, a competent exponent of the Filipino martial art, in the Warriors Eskrima, is defined as one who has the ability to neutralize an opponent. The specific skills required to achieve this goal are as follows:

- The ability not to get hit.
- The ability to disarm an opponent.
- The ability to immobilize an opponent.

The goal of training is expressed in the following phrases I introduced while conducting a seminar in London in 1992. These maxims are used as a verbal reinforcement while doing drills and exercises:

> Use a drill to instil a skill.
> Learn the skill and forget the drill.
> You fight with your skill not the drill.

Learning the techniques necessary for achieving skilfulness in the Filipino martial art is grounded on the Acquisition of Skills Triad. To achieve skilfulness in the Filipino martial arts, one must start with the acquisition of techniques that are solidly grounded on the fundamental principles of the Acquisition of Skills Triad. However, to gain mastery, one must transcend the mere acquisition of skills. The exponent of the art must try to reach an intellectual development ordered to synthesis – a dialectic.

A fight is won, due not only to skill but also, more importantly, to strategy. Techniques and physical prowess alone will not ensure one's survival in a life or death scenario. This factor is important when you consider that unlike during a training session, your opponent has real intent to harm you. In a conflict situation, one is confronted with an opponent who plans, thinks and may even be more skilled than you are. The strategy – formulated in terms of achieving effectiveness, efficiency and creativity – usually determines whether or not one prevails. What is needed at this level of development is not only the ability to perform the techniques mechanically in the most efficient manner but, more importantly, the ability to deal with opponent's strategy as well. The method of instruction used to attain this level of performance utilizes the 'Configuration Principle' – which unfortunately, for reasons of space, is not elaborated on here. It may, however, be found in the main work of the manuscript entitled, *A Philosophy of Filipino Martial Arts*.

The notion presented here of skills undergoing three stages of development is premised on the position we have taken that the weapon of the warrior is his mind – that the weapon in his hand or simply his hands alone are mere tools to achieve his goal. This has been inspired and influenced by two sources: the four stages of reading comprehension, and the 'Three dimensions of the becoming of our intellect' (*Retracing Reality*, 1999:77). What is needed at this level is not only the ability to perform the techniques in combination, but more importantly skilfulness, which means you have the ability to deal with the opponent's strategy, thereby allowing you to defeat him. A fight is won not only on skill but also on strategy.

The Appropriateness Principle

The main characteristic of the appropriateness principle is the ability to deliver the most effective technique when needed to neutralize the opponent. The ability to perform techniques efficiently would help, but what matters most is that the technique works. No well executed technique can save you when that technique does not work and does not neutralize the opponent's threat.

According to Socrates, the more you know, the more you know that you do not know. Therefore, the aim of the appropriateness principle is the deepening of knowledge as applied to practical situations. For one to survive in life-threatening situations the technique used must be effective – it must work. It is not difficult to imagine that not all techniques work every time, all the time. It is noted that a technique only works if it is appropriate to the circumstances and the demands of the situation. One trains to develop a skill that can hopefully be translated into an effective manoeuvre when needed. The actual threat to your life cannot be anticipated, so you train to develop abilities and attitudes that allow you to apply an effective manoeuvre when needed. There is no silver bullet, there is only a technique that will work effectively in any given situation or circumstance. Therefore, you need to respect other systems and develop an attitude of openness towards others.

The final principle is one of universality.

The Universality Principle

To establish the fundamentals of the Filipino martial art, one seeks what is common in the forms and styles and systems. It was noted that regardless of the origins of the system, the technique is applied to a common target – man. The attributes and characteristics of man on the physical level are universal. Therefore, despite the apparent differences in appearances, there must be a co-naturalness of the technique from one style to the other. Consequently, a technique that works when applied to someone using a stick should find a similar application with someone using a blade or a dagger. The science of biomechanics seems to support this hypothesis. Therefore, it is posited that techniques and practices when reduced to principles must have a common and universal applicability. This was noted in the implementation of the recommended programme to introduce the art to the educational system. In the Warriors system, the 'configuration' concept based on knife techniques of the Excalibur system is used to show students how the notion is applied to actual situations.

To a warrior, authority is the lamest of all reasons for using a technique. The technique learned must be performed at the highest level of efficiency otherwise it may not achieve its desired goal – technically speaking. The training methodology suggested for use by physical educators is to use the science of biomechanics. As such, the different *techniques* used in the many systems in use are reduced to a motor skill. The *motor* skill is then broken down to its basic element, and the desired sequence of training to facilitate learning is adopted. Performance of technique is then drilled to achieve fluidity using the correct mechanics to gain optimal performance. Then these skills are categorized according to fundamental movement patterns of the body.

The proposed structure now allows instruction to move from the traditional, highly individualized training programme to a system that allows it to be taught as a massed-based programme. Moreover, it no longer matters which particular style is used as an adjunct in classrooms all over the country. Techniques are viewed and taught as motor skills, like closed or open motor skills. Likewise, techniques are merely a series of fundamental movement patterns of the body, for example, locomotor and non-locomotor movements taught in physical education classes.

To recapitulate, any movement of a body can be described in a mechanistic manner as a fundamental movement pattern of the body. A fundamental movement pattern can then be analysed to facilitate training and instruction thereof. A fundamental movement pattern of the body oriented towards a particular goal or objective can be called a motor skill. Any fundamental movement pattern of the body or motor skill that can be used to deal with a particular situation is called a technique. A group of techniques categorized and ordered to conform to a particular way is deemed systematized, and is therefore called a system. A personal expression of a system to deal with particular situations is called a style.

Finally, the transformation of the traditional Filipino fighting art into a martial art is embodied in the Contention-Conflict-Cooperation Paradigm of the Warriors Eskrima system. The paradigm is the natural offshoot of Sun-Tzu's warning that fighting is never productive, while trying to live with the ancient maxim from an anonymous source that 'Man is best when he cooperates with the other'.

Students are drilled on the notion that while it is true that life involves struggle, this does not necessarily mean that it should end in conflict. What is suggested is that any contentious situation should be approached through discourse and not with argumentation. Aristotle admonishes that when two people argue then you have two confused people.

Students should strive to achieve cooperation with the other. However, if this is not possible, then all efforts should be exerted to settle for a compromise: at least a compromise would keep the possibility of cooperation on the horizon. Conflict should be avoided at all cost. However, aggressive behaviour and violence is a practical reality in life. Therefore, a benefit of training in the Filipino martial art is that while one is developing desirable traits and attitudes, the student also develops a skill – a fundamental movement pattern of the body, which can be utilized to deal with threats to one's life by using one's creativity in crafting and manipulating implements for defensive purposes.

The Warriors Eskrima's methodology of teaching uses a device with the 'infinity' sign as an inspiration. This methodology was the outcome of a focused discussion made with Mr Orville Visitacion, a painter and a fellow eskrimador, while undertaking my research for my dissertation. The final form, which eventually came to be known as the *Phases of Learning*, was influenced by three sources, namely: the Stages of Reading Comprehension Model, the 'infinity sign' of mathematics and its significance, and the philosophical notion of Marie-Dominique Philippe's three dimensions of intellectual development that corresponds neatly with the three qualities of skills' acquisitions of various repertoires of 'techniques' as a Filipino martial artist.

Mr Orville Visitacion was kind enough to illustrate the three stages of development in training of the Filipino martial art. The graphic illustration he has made is shown (*below*), with corresponding elucidation and elaboration. It may be worth noting here that in the Warriors Eskrima, the weapon of the warrior is the 'mind'. The stages of development are represented by the 'Figure 8' pattern, the 'Figure X' pattern and the 'Vector' pattern.

The 'Figure 8' Pattern

A continuous execution of a forehand and a backhand slash describes an easily recognizable 'Figure 8' pattern. The movement may be described as a general waving of the arm motion. While the performer thinks that he is executing distinct forehand and backhand strikes to an imaginary opponent, to an astute observer the beginner is essentially executing a Figure 8 pattern of strike, without any definite focus on where the power is delivered. This constitutes the first phase of learning. A graphic illustration of the movement follows:

GM Pasa – 'figure 8' pattern.

LEFT: GM Pasa – 'figure X' pattern.

BELOW: GM Pasa – 'vector' pattern.

The 'Figure X' Pattern

In the second phase of learning, the performer recognizes that the force of the strike needs to be focused. As a result, the forehand and backhand strikes are executed with more authority and power. The power of the blow is observed to be delivered in the strike within the body of the imaginary opponent, and the loops of the forehand and the backhand strike are now observed to be without any force or power – they now become what may be termed as the recovery phase of the blow.

The new pattern may be better appreciated in graphic form as shown (*above*), rather than by description, and would look like a Figure X to a knowledgeable observer.

The 'Vector' Pattern

The third and final phase of learning may be best represented by the graphic illustration, as shown (*right*).

The Phases of Learning

Pattern	Technical Aspects	Intellectual Development
'Figure 8'	Efficiency	Extension ordered to quantitative development
'Figure X'	Effectiveness	Penetration ordered to qualitative development
'Vector'	Adaptation	Artistic efficiency ordered to synthesis

The obvious flow of force on the strike has become shorter. This is the result of the recognition that as soon as the strike reaches the intended point of impact, the force in the blow needs to be immediately withheld in preparation to the next blow. The recovery phase therefore becomes shorter. As a consequence, more strikes can be executed within a specified period of time than is possible in the previous two patterns of movement. The practical result of this is that the strike becomes more responsive to actual conditions of combat, where the ability to execute strikes quickly becomes critical.

The various elements involved in the phases of learning are shown in the table above.

The Figure 8 pattern of movement is linked to the characteristic of the development of a motor skill, where the correct mechanical performance in terms of form and sequence of a technique is a primary consideration. Therefore, the task of skill acquisition is aimed at developing efficiency in performance. While this stage of learning is characterized by efficiency in performance, the corresponding stage of intellectual development is described by Marie-Dominique Philippe as an extension of knowledge ordered to quantitative development – in ordinary language, the attempt by the student to learn as many techniques as he can with the expectation that more is better, to better prepare him to deal with any and all exigencies.

The second stage, the Figure X pattern of movement, on the other hand, focuses more on the dimension of effectiveness of technique in practical situations. The motor skills thus acquired are now fine-tuned. The ability to generate power, speed and accuracy becomes more important at this stage. The ability to execute combinations of various techniques also becomes central to the training exercises. The stage of intellectual development now shifts from extension (a viewpoint aimed toward the horizon) to penetration (a view aimed toward the deepening of understanding) of knowledge ordered towards qualitative development. In ordinary language, the student now starts to discern which of the techniques learned are most likely to work for him in real crisis situations. The criterion is more of whether these techniques will work, and not one based on how nice it makes one look.

The final stage of development, the Vector pattern of movement, moves toward the development of strategy. Acquired skills are now honed with a view towards adaptation – adaptation in the sense that one cannot possibly know what actual techniques he would need in real life-threatening scenarios. No one has the gift of providence. We cannot know in advance what we will need to deal with our future: we can only prepare. This stage of development of skills acquisition is described by Marie-Dominique Philippe, a philosopher and theologian, as the stage of intellectual development aimed at synthesis.

13 Reasonable Force: Self-Defence and the Law

British law allows 'such force as is reasonable in the circumstances' to be applied against an attacker, whether in self-defence or in defence of another. That sounds all very well, but consider not only how varied the 'circumstances' may be, but also how many opinions there could be about how to interpret the word 'reasonable'. What does this mean for you, in practical terms?

In the following discussion, the words 'he' and 'him' are used for the attacker. Nothing sexist is implied here, simply the practical recognition that far more physical assaults are by males than females. The law and the attitudes remain the same, whatever the number or sex of your assailants.

Let us consider the following aspects:

- Your options and immediate reactions to the situation.
- Witnesses.
- Consequences.
- Weapons.
- Attitudes.

Reactions

You may have a situation that you can 'see coming', in that someone is becoming increasingly angry, or approaching you, or there are threats and demands before physical action. Alternatively, you may be surprised by an attack, and your trained response will be quick, and more 'instinctive' than if it were under any conscious control. However, if there is any thinking time before physical conflict, what are your options?

Escape

The traditional approach for any martial arts teacher is to tell you that if you can escape from a situation of potential physical danger, then you must do so. Of course you should. There is no dishonour in avoiding physical conflict with some anti-social person whom you are unfortunate enough to encounter. On the contrary, it is both moral and intelligent, because neither of you is physically damaged, and he may be armed, and much more ruthless and dangerous than you imagine.

Escape may not be an option. This could be simply because the threat is blocking your only possible escape route (in which case you should really have been more aware of your surroundings in the first place, rather than being in a situation where you are vulnerable to such a trap).

Another scenario is that you could be on the other side of the street, well away from personal danger, when you see an old lady being mugged. No one else can have your conscience or your attitudes about getting involved in such a situation. No one else will live with your feelings if you walk away from that. You may be inexperienced at martial arts, or it could be that you can see that the situation involves bigger and/or multiple attackers, and your judgement is that if you get involved, there will just be one more injured body rather than a rescued old lady, and it would be much wiser for you to make a noise, try and worry them enough to run off, and call the police. Always try and use your brains before your fists.

Alternatively you could go over there and hope that what they are after is a victim rather than a fight. This is often the case: people involved in street violence are trying to inflict it, not suffer it themselves. They may then decide to run for it and find themselves another victim another day. Or you may be involved in the necessary use of physical force.

Negotiate

I shall use this word in a wide sense, of 'using words to defuse or get out of the situation', not in the narrower sense of a deal or compromise of some sort. This may mean that he is angry, and that *you must not get angry*. Anger will only fuel the situation and increase the chances of physical conflict. You may be frightened, and you have to be ready for action: that is not at all the same as being angry. If possible, always try and defuse the situation. Use non-threatening words and gestures, rather than aggressive expressions or body language, while remaining ready to move if necessary.

It may also mean that he asks for your wallet and your credit cards, and you give them to him. This may be all he wants, and he may then go away. Let it go, always: this is better than the risk of injury or death to either or both of you. It is not a betrayal of your faith in yourself as a martial artist: your belief should be that if you had to fight him, he will end up far worse off than you. You should never feel the need to prove this because of 'pride'. If you *know* you are better than he is at dealing with physical conflict, then the pride is in *avoiding* it: because if you engage in it, he will become the victim, not you. You are no longer the 'defender' in any meaningful sense, but simply a bully. Know this inside, and let it go.

However, in an apparent robbery situa-tion, do not ever make the mistake of 'letting down your guard'. Some people will use robbery as an excuse for the opportunity to inflict violence on a victim. This may mean either that you give him what he wants and then you still have to defend yourself anyway; or that he tries to hurt you first, and then would take belongings from you as a 'bonus' rather than as a primary motive for the encounter.

The essential point here is that if you either escape or 'negotiate' your way out of the situation, the worst you have to deal with is cancelling your credit cards and making reports to the police. No charges can have been brought against you; there is no physical injury, whether temporary or permanent; there is no question of anyone scrutinizing whether your 'use of force' was 'reasonable', because you got out of the situation without the use of any physical force. All you have been is unlucky.

The other options involve physical conflict. Now it is *possible* that he could assault you and then back away. For example, angry words are followed by shoving you into a wall or another person, but then, not really wanting to fight, he withdraws. He will probably be swearing, but you must learn to let verbal aggression wash over you, as it is irrelevant: if he is letting off steam, you do not have to care. It is far preferable to the potential effects of physical aggression.

In such a circumstance, you again *must not* get angry. You must also not have the belief that you are now 'entitled' to fight him, as 'he started it', because you are not: as far as the law is concerned, your appropriate course of action is to bring a charge of assault against him. If you go after him, it is considered revenge, *not* self-defence, because you have then become the aggressor, and no matter how unjust you may personally think this is, *he* is entitled to bring charges of assault against *you*.

On the other hand, when the situation 'kicks off' physically, there may be no question of *him* removing the attack unless he receives sufficient discouragement. Your responsibility then, in the eyes of the law, is to use only minimal force to remove the attack or restrain the attacker, and then to disengage from the conflict.

Witnesses

Physical conflict happens in many different circumstances. Someone looking for a victim on a quiet street at night is likely to deliberately arrange to confront you in a place where there are no witnesses. On the other hand, a fight can of course take place in or outside a pub or nightclub.

If there are no witnesses, you can end up with a situation which is 'your word against his'. Who started it? What happened? You cannot expect him to say 'It's a fair cop, guv', and to confess to the police if he thinks he can instead sue you for assault. The less reasonable and restrained your response, the greater the danger that you have clearly used 'unreasonable' force, even if you can convince people that you did not initiate the problem.

You might think that witnesses would be 'on your side'. You live a respectable life, you are minding your own business, and someone else starts trouble. If it is the kind of situation where it 'builds up', then independent witnesses can be vital, *as long as* you were clearly demonstrating that you were 'trying to talk him down' and that you 'did not want to fight'. Memories are fickle and faulty. If you are in any way angry or aggressive, and this is seen by others, then there is more likely to be some reinterpretation of the situation – in front of a jury months later.

Witnesses may, of course, work against you rather than for you. First, they may be friends or acquaintances of the defeated attacker. Second, in some circumstances it is *probable* rather than possible that independent witnesses simply do not see his first physical assault on you, but perhaps catch a

movement with their peripheral vision and turn to see *your* physical reaction against him. In other words, it looks to them as if you acted first, rather than in self-defence.

Consequences

The problem is that the consequences of physical conflict are unpredictable. You could knock someone down in the street, and they hit their head on the kerb and die. But even if no one dies, if you 'win' a physical encounter, then by definition he is likely to end up more damaged than you are; by definition, you could be said to have used more force than he has. (The only real way to 'win' is by escape or 'negotiation'.)

He may be an experienced criminal from a socially disadvantaged background, used to living a life of lies and aggression and resentment. If in a condition to do so, he is likely to tell lies about *you*, and quite possibly you will end up facing charges of assault brought by *him*. If he has not survived the encounter, you are open to charges of manslaughter or even murder.

All of these possibilities mean that your bad luck did not 'end' when you survived the encounter. Months later, perhaps after your (and/or his) injuries have healed, you could be in the cold light of a courtroom, with lawyers and jurors examining in great detail whether any force you used – perhaps quickly and under great stress – could be justified as 'reasonable in the circumstances'.

You have to remember that only a tiny minority of lawyers or jurors have any real understanding of martial arts. A 'jury of your peers' means the equivalent of twelve ordinary people chosen at random from off the street. They will undoubtedly have picked up misconceptions about martial arts from popular culture, and may very well regard you as 'dangerous'. When it is known that you have any martial arts training at all, you will inevitably be regarded as a 'martial arts expert', with skills that they may regard with suspicion. There will not be any newspaper reports describing you as 'an adequate or moderate student of martial arts'!

That makes it harder for you, not easier. As a martial artist, therefore, you have more responsibility, not less, to exercise restraint and avoid conflict. You have to face the fact that it will be more difficult for you to justify that you believed that you (or another person) were in immediate danger, and that in order to prevent yourself, or them, being physically harmed, you used only enough force that was reasonable in the circumstances, to remove the threat.

Weapons

The presence or use of weapons, apart from increasing the danger of severe injury or death, can have a serious effect on the perception of 'reasonable' force.

If the attacker is unarmed, and you use something available as a weapon against him (such as a piece of wood or a bar stool), then you would have a difficult time arguing that you have used only 'reasonable' force. If he is armed, and you are not, then your defensive actions can be rather more serious and still be regarded as 'reasonable'. That is, however, a very general observation, and an actual situation will be complicated by circumstances, injuries suffered by any involved party, counter-claims by the attacker, and the actual nature and use of any weapon involved (whether by him or, if you take it from him, by you).

You will be in trouble, and will receive no sympathy from police or the courts, if you were carrying something that was intended to be used as a weapon. This applies even if you have never drawn this item in anger, and even if you only ever intended to use it in a 'self-defence' situation.

This does not only apply to items *designed* to cause injury, such as a knife, razor or knuckleduster. A screwdriver, for example, was not designed to cause injury, but if you are carrying one, with no associated justification provided by the nature of your trade, but carrying it for 'defensive purposes', then it is still an item '*intended* to cause injury'.

The legal position is simple: if you are a law-abiding citizen in Britain, you do not carry anything intended to be used as a weapon.

This does not make you incapable of using an appropriate awareness of the possibilities of hitting someone with an umbrella, or using, say, a pen or car keys as a projectile distraction while you escape: you may be hitting a mugger in the face with something, but clearly it was not something carried with the intention of causing injury. That is the significant difference.

Attitudes

As you can see, even leaving aside the difficulties of applying actual techniques while in danger and under stress, you cannot underestimate two aspects of the potential consequences of physical encounters:

- their unpredictability (for example, permanent crippling injury or a counter-claim of assault against you);
- their seriousness (for example, a drawn-out legal dispute and a prison sentence for *you*).

As a martial artist, you have an increased responsibility to acquire emotional control and to exercise restraint. Becoming the victim of someone else wanting to inflict violence on you is most unfortunate, but becoming the victim of your own anger or fear should be avoidable. This is not, however, a reason for *avoiding* acquiring martial arts skills! Suppose you were given a choice of two consequences:

- Having no defensive skills, you happen to die in a street encounter. You are remembered as an innocent victim, and you leave behind grieving relatives and friends.

Or:

- In an unavoidable street encounter, your skills ensure you survive without permanent injury. Months later, you are putting up with the stress of trying to justify whether the force you used in a dark street against an unprovoked attack was 'reasonable', to people who have terribly respectable lives and have not been in a fight since they were nine years old. You are even under the threat of a prison sentence for assault. But you know you only did what you had to at the time, and you are doing what you can to continue living a good life.

Which is preferable? Your first priority is to survive and protect others as well as yourself, and one way of 'protecting' your loved ones is protecting them from grief over your unnecessary loss.

Fundamentally, your responsibility is always to 'survive and protect' *within the boundaries of the law.*

In Conclusion

In summary, there will always be good and bad luck involved, but if you want to maximize the chances of not falling foul of the law, the attitudes to cultivate are:

- Do not go around looking for trouble.
- You do not have anything to prove.
- If trouble finds you, show that you *do not want to fight*, and do what you can to avoid physical conflict.
- Only use physical techniques if you have absolutely no choice.
- Then be as restrained as possible in the circumstances.
- Never strike the assailant after the direct threat has been removed. Remember, you are one of the 'good guys', not one of the criminals.

Appendix
Understanding Anatomy

Even if we concentrate largely on the **blood vessels**, rather than going into detail about internal organs, it is quickly appreciated how many life-threatening targets there are in many parts of the body, and how extremely serious the potential consequences of a knife attack can be. Therefore, a certain amount of knowledge about anatomy can only help to underline the importance of learning how to efficiently protect specific targets from knife attack.

Perhaps the fundamental starting point is to appreciate what the blood vessels do, and what they are for. Respiration (breathing) takes in oxygen from the air, which diffuses into the **arterial** blood through capillaries (tiny blood vessels) in the lungs. At the same time carbon dioxide enters the lungs from the waste-rich blood from the **veins**.

As the heart pumps, it pushes the oxygen-rich blood through the arteries, supplying all parts of the body with oxygen in this way. Once the oxygen has been extracted by the cells and muscles for use in the metabolic processes, the blood (now drained of oxygen and carrying the waste product of carbon dioxide) returns to the heart and lungs through the veins.

This is why a cut to a vein may cause blood only to flow out, whereas a cut to an artery, 'pushed' by the pumping of the heart, may pulse or gush out, leading to quicker and more serious blood loss.

The Veins of the Neck

The external jugular: This vein is the pathway of blood from the exterior of the skull and the interior of the face. It starts on a level with the angle of the lower jaw, in the parotid gland; this is the largest of the salivary glands, and is in front of (and below) the ear.

The external jugular follows a line drawn to the middle of the clavicle (collar-bone). It crosses the **sterno-cleido-mastoid** muscle; this muscle has two heads, at the sternum (breast-bone) and clavicle, which blend below the middle of the neck into one muscle, which inserts at the top into the mastoid process (the bone at the side and base of the skull) below and behind the ear.

The internal jugular: This vein is the pathway of blood from the inside of the skull, the surface of the face and the neck. It starts at the base of the skull, and the top part of this vein is quite large (dilated). It runs vertically down the side of the neck, at first behind and on the *outer* side of the **internal carotid artery**, then on the outer side of the **common carotid** (*see below* for further explanation of these terms).

It unites with the **subclavian vein** at the root of the neck where the sternum and the clavicle join.

The middle thyroid vein: This vein collects the blood from the lower part of the side of the thyroid gland (at the upper part of the trachea, or windpipe). It goes into the lower part of the **internal jugular**.

The carotid arteries: These arteries are not symmetrical. Blood from the left side of the heart is pumped up into the **aorta**, which starts as an arch going up and then down behind the heart near the backbone. The **left common carotid** and the **left subclavian** arteries come directly up out of the left side of the arch of the aorta.

However, only one artery leaves the right side of the arch; this is the brachiocephalic artery, which is only about 1.8–2.4in (45–60cm) long. This then branches into the **right common carotid** and the **right subclavian** arteries.

The origin of the left common carotid, below the root of the neck, is therefore deeper within the body than the origin of the right common carotid.

The carotid arteries then rise from behind where the sternum and clavicle join, and pass obliquely (angling outwards) upwards to a point midway between the angle of the jaw and the mastoid process. At a level immediately above the Adam's apple it divides, separated by both muscles and nerves, into the **external** and **internal carotids**.

The **common carotid** (the lower part, before the branching) is quite deeply seated, covered by muscles and cartilage. It is contained in a sheath of tissue, which also encloses a nerve (the pneumogastric nerve) and the internal jugular vein (which is on the outside). The middle thyroid vein crosses it at its centre.

The **external carotid** distributes blood to the outside of the head and face. It is closest to the surface where it branches from the common carotid, and then higher up it passes more deeply into the parotid gland.

The **internal carotid** supplies blood to the inside of the skull, the front of the brain and the eye.

The left subclavian artery: This artery is deeper in the chest cavity than the right. Both of them are also behind muscles and nerves. The internal jugular passes in front of them. The subclavian artery then passes behind the **brachial plexus** of nerves. At the lower border of the first rib, still behind the brachial plexus, it becomes the axillary artery. This starts quite deep, but is closer to the surface where it becomes the **brachial artery**.

The Arteries and Nerves of the Arm

The brachial artery: This artery starts at the lower margin of the tendon of the teres major (a muscle starting from the bottom of the shoulder blade and angling upwards to a tendon inserted into the back of the humerus, the large bone of the upper arm).

From the armpit it runs down the inside of the arm and then curves into the inner elbow, ending about half an inch below the elbow (where it branches into the **radial** and **ulnar** arteries). It is quite near the surface throughout its length, being only slightly overlapped by the biceps.

The brachial plexus: This is a group of nerves extending from the lower part of the side of the neck, running below the clavicle to the armpit. The branches above the collar bone relate to the neck, and the back and side of the chest. Below the collar bone it divides into three cords, at first surrounding the axillary artery, then dividing into three branches that send nerves to the front of the chest and the shoulder, and six branches supplying the various parts of the hand and arm. It divides opposite the coracoid process (a thick curved piece of bone at the top of the shoulder blade).

The Arteries and Muscles of the Forearm and Inner Wrist

The radial artery: This artery runs quite

near the surface of the forearm to the thumb side of the wrist (then around the thumb and into the palm), with **flexor** muscles to the inside of it and under it, but also, in its upper two thirds, a **supinator** muscle on top of it.

The ulnar artery: This artery runs down to the little finger side (and into the palm), but it is set deeper, below many of the **flexor** muscles.

The **extensor** muscles, several of them, are on the back of the forearm.

The **flexor** muscles enable us to close the fist and to hold a weapon; the **supinator** muscles enable us to turn the hand over. The **extensor** muscles enable us to open the hand and extend the fingers. Therefore, a cut to the extensor muscles on the back of the arm may still leave you capable of holding a weapon or clenching a fist, whereas a cut to the flexor muscles on the inner wrist may make this impossible.

The Arteries of the Lower Body

As supplementary information to the following, the **vertebrae** are the bones of the spinal column. Starting at the top, there are:

- seven cervical vertebrae;
- twelve dorsal vertebrae (*see* ⋆ in 'abdominal aorta' below);
- five lumbar vertebrae (*see* ⋆ 'abdominal aorta' below);
- five fused vertebrae of the sacrum;
- four fused vertebrae of the coccyx.

The **diaphragm** (*see* ⋆ in 'abdominal aorta' below) is the muscle fibre separating the chest from the abdomen; it assists with the process of breathing.

The **abdominal aorta** starts at the aortic opening of the diaphragm⋆, immediately in front of the last dorsal⋆ vertebra. It runs

down, behind the stomach, pancreas and duodenum, slightly to the left of the vertebral column, terminating to the left of the fourth lumbar⋆ vertebra, at the level of the umbilicus (belly button), where it divides into the **common iliac arteries**.

The common iliac: This artery is only about 2in (5cm) long and then divides into the **internal iliac** (supplying the guts and pelvis) and the **external iliac** (supplying the legs and feet).

The external iliac: This artery runs to the middle of the hip crease; where it enters the thigh it becomes the **femoral artery**.

The femoral artery: The femoral runs down towards the inner side of the knee. It is quite near the surface in the upper third of the thigh. In the middle third it is more deeply buried by muscle. In the lower third it becomes the popliteal artery, supplying the lower leg. (The popliteal artery divides into the anterior and posterior tibial arteries, passing in front of and behind the tibia (shin bone) down to the ankle and foot.)

The Practical Implications for Knife Defence

To combine this information with practical concerns, the first thing to appreciate is that all over the body there are targets of life-threatening vulnerability: it is virtually impossible to stab someone with the intention of hurting them *without* killing them, except perhaps in the foot. If you survive a stab wound it is because you are lucky, rather than because it is not near a vital target. If you find the victim of a knife attack it is essential to check their breathing and circulation and to get them professional medical attention without delay.

Developing good, sensible knife defence technique is essential. It may indeed be the case that if someone with a knife is determined to hurt you, you are going to get cut, but you need to ensure that your training minimizes the exposure of deadly targets and maximizes the concept of exposing less dangerous targets while attempting to control the knife, and disarm the attacker, or counter attack. Remember that:

- Any knife wound to the neck area is extremely serious. For you, it must be avoided; for others, it must be treated without delay.
- A wound to the front of the shoulder looks to the unaware like a 'relatively safe' thrust to take, but it can (a) remove the use of the arm and hand, which are controlled by the brachial plexus of nerves; and it can (b) even be fatal, by penetrating the subclavian artery and/or a lung.
- Cuts to the brachial artery (inner arm) or femoral artery (inner thigh) are fortunately rare but they are immediately life-threatening.
- Over half of knife attack wounds are to the abdominal and chest areas, with a large number of internal organs as well as major blood vessels endangered.
- Where there is a stab wound there is likely to be serious internal bleeding as well as, or instead of, visible external bleeding.
- Protecting the inner forearms can be important for a whole range of possible reasons. Severed flexor muscles means that you cannot make a fist, or grab or hold an item to use either as a shield or a weapon, or pick up a phone or radio to call for help.

Understanding what the muscles do should lead to a greater appreciation of what may happen in a confrontation. For example, there have been situations in which a defender, trained and trying to control the knife wielded by his attacker, has actually grabbed hold of the knife. When the police turn up and tell him to drop the knife, he is incapable of doing so, because another cut to the back of his forearm has severed his extensor muscles and he cannot open his hand.

It is extremely important to appreciate that techniques originating from empty-hand defence methods, and concepts such as 'taking a punch', are utterly inappropriate where edged weapons are concerned. To increase your statistical chances of surviving a knife attack, and to be armed with appropriate knowledge, the following advice is the best that you could be given:

- Get functional weapons-orientated martial arts training from a qualified instructor.
- Understand that nothing will improve your survival chances to 100 per cent, and a grading certificate does not control the accidents of destiny. Work intelligently and persistently on your own progress and abilities.
- Learn something of how the muscles and the body work, as well as learning martial arts techniques.
- Do a First Aid course. Your skills will not help someone who could be dying if you encounter the victim of an attack after the attacker has disappeared. The responsibilities of the warrior extend beyond simply being able to protect him or herself.
- Don't carry a knife. Look at the havoc it can cause to a human body.

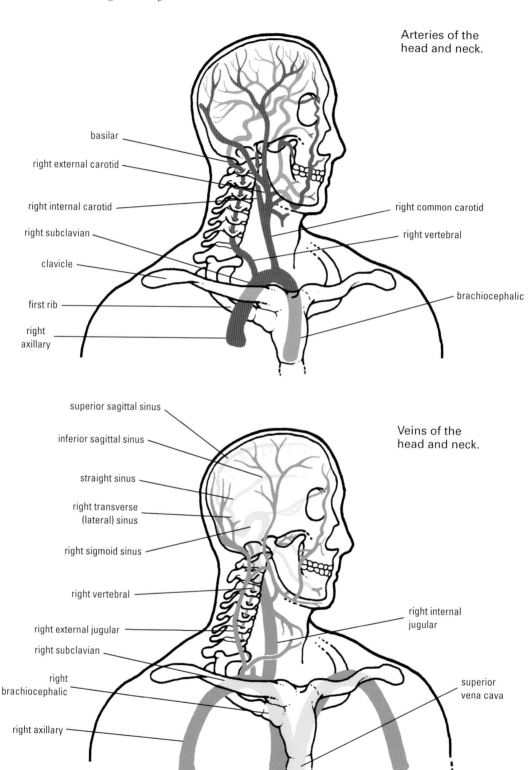

Arteries of the
head and neck.

basilar

right external carotid

right internal carotid

right subclavian

clavicle

first rib

right
axillary

right common carotid

right vertebral

brachiocephalic

Veins of the
head and neck.

superior sagittal sinus

inferior sagittal sinus

straight sinus

right transverse
(lateral) sinus

right sigmoid sinus

right vertebral

right external jugular

right subclavian

right
brachiocephalic

right axillary

right internal
jugular

superior
vena cava

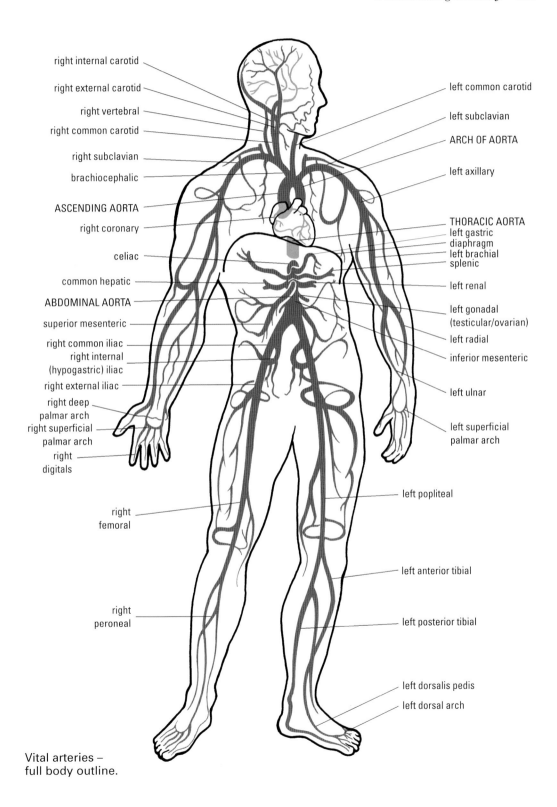

right internal carotid

right external carotid

right vertebral

right common carotid

right subclavian

brachiocephalic

ASCENDING AORTA

right coronary

celiac

common hepatic

ABDOMINAL AORTA

superior mesenteric

right common iliac

right internal
(hypogastric) iliac

right external iliac

right deep
palmar arch

right superficial
palmar arch

right
digitals

right
femoral

right
peroneal

left common carotid

left subclavian

ARCH OF AORTA

left axillary

THORACIC AORTA
left gastric
diaphragm
left brachial
splenic

left renal

left gonadal
(testicular/ovarian)

left radial

inferior mesenteric

left ulnar

left superficial
palmar arch

left popliteal

left anterior tibial

left posterior tibial

left dorsalis pedis

left dorsal arch

Vital arteries –
full body outline.

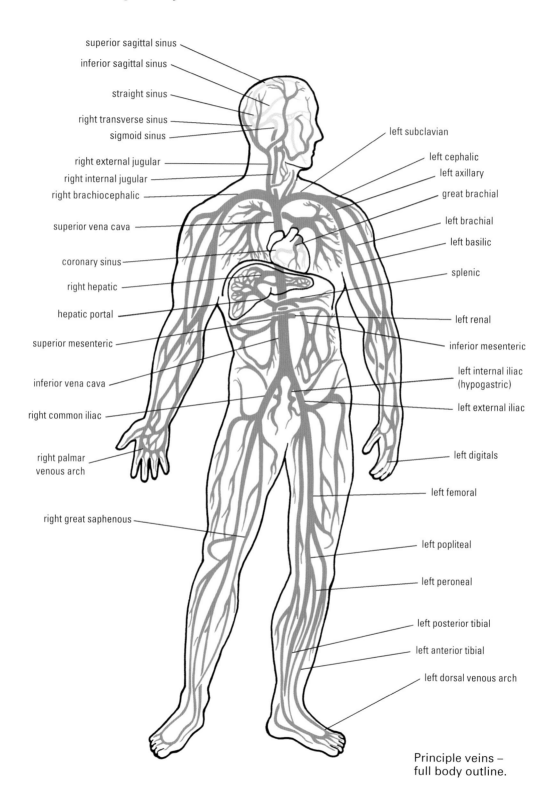

superior sagittal sinus

inferior sagittal sinus

straight sinus

right transverse sinus

sigmoid sinus

right external jugular

right internal jugular

right brachiocephalic

superior vena cava

coronary sinus

right hepatic

hepatic portal

superior mesenteric

inferior vena cava

right common iliac

right palmar
venous arch

right great saphenous

left subclavian

left cephalic

left axillary

great brachial

left brachial

left basilic

splenic

left renal

inferior mesenteric

left internal iliac
(hypogastric)

left external iliac

left digitals

left femoral

left popliteal

left peroneal

left posterior tibial

left anterior tibial

left dorsal venous arch

Principle veins –
full body outline.

Further Information

Suggested Reading

The following is not a complete bibliography, but a detailed list of historical works on the Philippines, and instructional books on the Filipino martial arts.

Canete, Dionisio A., *Eskrima, Kali, Arnis* (Cebu City: Doce Pares Publishing House Inc., 1993)

Canete, Ciriaco C. and Pares, Doce, *Basic Eskrima-Arnis-Kali-Pangolisi* (Cebu City: Doce Pares Publishing House Inc., 1989)

Canete, Eulogio Snr *et al*, *Arnis (Eskrima) Philippines' Stickfighting Art* (Cebu City: Doce Pares Publishing Inc., 1976)

Cody, Mark E. and Dionaldo, Ray, *Filipino Combat Systems* (Florida: Authorhouse, 2005)

Diego Antonio and Ricketts, Christopher, *The Secrets of Kalis Ilustrisimo* (Rutland, Vermont: Charles E. Tuttle Co., 2002)

Galang, Reynaldo S., *Classic Arnis - The Legacy of Placido Yambao* (New Jersey: Arjee Enterprises, 2004)

Galang, Reynaldo S., *Masters of the Blade* (New Jersey: Arjee Enterprises, 2006)

Galang, Reynaldo S., *Warrior Arts of the Philippines* (New Jersey: Bakbakan International, 2006)

Hurley, Vic, *Swish of the Kris: The story of the Moros* (Bangkok: Orchid Press, 2008)

Inosanto, Dan and Johnson, Gilber R., *The Filipino Martial Arts* (Los Angeles: Know How Publishing Co., 1980)

Lema, Benjamin Luna, *Arnis: The Filipino Art of Self Defense* (Pasig, Metro Manila: Integrated Publishing House, 1989)

Marinas, Amante P., *Panandata Dalawang Yantok (Arnis Double Sticks Fighting)* (San Juan, Philippines: Socorro Publications, 1987)

Pasa, Abner G., *Filipino Martial Arts Basic Training Manual* (Cebu City: Institute of Filipino Martial Arts of Cebu, Inc., 1997)

Pasa, Abner G., *Fundamental Principles and Theories of the Filipino Martial Arts* (Cebu City: Institute of Filipino Martial Arts of Cebu, Inc., 1997)

Pasa, Abner G., *The Mechanics of Arnis for Physical Educators, 2nd Edition* (Cebu City: Balitok Publishing, 2002)

Presas, Remy, *Makabagong Arnis De Mano* (Quezon City: Modern Arnis Publishing Co., 1974)

Presas, Remy, *The Practical Art of Eskrima, 2nd Edition* (Quezon City: National Book Store Inc., 1994)

Quirino, Carlos, *Filipinos at War* (Philippines: Vera Reyes Inc.)

Reid, Howard and Croucher, Michael, *The Way of the Warrior* (London: Century Publishing, 1983)

Scott, William Henry, *Barangay - Sixteenth Century Philippine Culture and Society* (Quezon City: Ateneo de Manila University Press, 1994)

Scott, William Henry, *Looking for the Prehispanic Filipino* (Quezon City: Ateneo de Manila University Press, 1994)

Somera, Tony, *The Secrets of Giron Arnis-Eskrima* (Rutland, Vermont: Charles E. Tuttle Co., 1998)

Sulite, Edgar G., *Masters of Arnis, Kali & Eskrima* (Philippines: Socorro Publications, 1993)

Sulite, Edgar G., *The Secrets of Arnis* (Philippines: Socorro Publications, 1993)

Wiley, Mark V., *Arnis: History & Methods of Filipino Martial Arts* (Rutland, Vermont: Charles E. Tuttle Co., 2001)

Wiley, Mark V., *Filipino Fighting Arts* (California: Unique Publications, 2001)

Wiley, Mark V., *Filipino Martial Arts, Cabales Serrada Eskrima* (Rutland, Vermont: Charles E. Tuttle Co., 1994)

Wiley, Mark V., *Filipino Martial Culture* (Rutland, Vermont: Charles E. Tuttle Co., 1997)

Zaide, Gregorio F., *Documentary Sources of Philippine History, Vol. 1* (Manila: National Book Store, 1990)

Zaide, Sonia M., *The Philippines: A Unique Nation* (Quezon City: All Nations Publishing Co. Inc., 1994)

Websites

Styles
www.warriors-eskrima.co.uk
www.balitok.com
www.sayoc.com

Merchandise
www.fma-equipment.com

Councils
www.kali-sports.com

Forums
www.fmatalk.com
www.fmaforum.org

Tournaments
www.wekafgb.com
www.arnisphilippines.com

Online Magazine
www.fmadigest.com

Index